Dana Carleton Munro, Edith Bramhall

The Early Christian Persecutions

Dana Carleton Munro, Edith Bramhall

The Early Christian Persecutions

ISBN/EAN: 9783337258856

Printed in Europe, USA, Canada, Australia, Japan

Cover: Foto ©ninafisch / pixelio.de

More available books at **www.hansebooks.com**

Translations and Reprints

FROM THE

Original Sources of European History

THE EARLY CHRISTIAN PERSECUTIONS.

Edited by Dana Carleton Munro, A.M., and Edith Bramhall, A.M.

PUBLISHED BY

The Department of History of the University of Pennsylvania.

Philadelphia, Pa., 1897.

English Agency: P. S. KING & SON, 12-14 King Street, London, S. W.

Price, 20 Cents.

THE use of original contemporary sources, or of documents on which our knowledge of history is so largely based, has come to be valued in recent times at something like its true worth. The sequence of past events, the form and spirit of institutions, the characters of men, the prevailing habits of thought, obtain their greatest reality when we study them in the very words used by the men to whom the past was the living present. Even historians who have not been characterized by a close dependence on the results of patient investigation of the sources have recognized the superiority of an appeal to original testimony. Mr. Froude says, "Whenever possible, let us not be told about this man or that. Let us hear the man himself speak, let us see him act, and let us be left to form our own opinion about him." And in "Stones of Venice," Mr. Ruskin writes, "the only history worth reading is that written at the time of which it treats, the history of what was done and seen, heard out of the mouths of the men who did and saw. One fresh draught of such history is worth more than a thousand volumes of abstracts, and reasonings, and suppositions and theories."

Experience has proved, not only that the interest of students can be more readily obtained through the vividness of a direct and first-hand presentation, and that knowledge thus gained is more tangible and exact; but that the critical judgment is developed in no slight degree, and the ability as well as the interest for further study thus secured.

The utilization of the original sources of history has, however, been much restricted by their comparative inaccessibility. A great proportion of such documents as illustrate European history exist only in more or less unfamiliar languages; many are to be found only in large and expensive collections, or in works that are out of print and therefore difficult to obtain or consult.

The desire to overcome in some degree this inaccessibility, especially for their own classes, led the editors of the present series of translations and reprints from the original sources of European history to undertake its publication. During the past three years evidence has been given of the usefulness of the documents in several directions. Their most considerable use has naturally been with college classes. One or more of the issues has been used in twenty-two of the principal Universities and Colleges. In addition to these and their use in lower schools they have been found to give increased value to University Extension courses and reading circles.

During the coming year the series will consist of five "double numbers" of 32 pages or more, each. The separate numbers will be edited respectively by Dana Carleton Munro, A.M. and Edith Bramhall, A.M., of the University of Pennsylvania, Edwin Knox Mitchell, of Hartford Theological Seminary, Edward P. Cheyney, A.M., of the University of Pennsylvania, Arthur C. Howland, Ph. D., of the University of Illinois, and Merrick Whitcomb, Ph.D., of the University of Pennsylvania. Titles of the numbers and further particulars are given on the third cover page.

Translations and Reprints

FROM THE

ORIGINAL SOURCES OF EUROPEAN HISTORY.

| VOL. IV. | THE EARLY CHRISTIAN PERSECUTIONS. | No. 1. |

TABLE OF CONTENTS.

		PAGE
I.	INTRODUCTION,	2
	Tertullian's general statement,	2
II.	PERSECUTION UNDER NERO.	
	Account by Tacitus,	4
	Account by Suetonius,	5
	Account by Clement,	5
	Account by Sulpicius Severus,	6
III.	PERSECUTION UNDER DOMITIAN.	
	The Flavian Policy—Sulpicious Severus,	6
	Account by Dio Cassius,	7
	Account by Suetonius,	7
IV.	ATTITUDE OF TRAJAN AND HADRIAN.	
	Pliny's Letter to Trajan,	8
	Trajan's Reply,	9
	Hadrian's Rescript to Minucius Fundanus,	10
V.	PERSECUTION UNDER MARCUS AURELIUS.	
	Martyrdoms at Lyons and Vienna,	11
VI.	PERSECUTIONS OF THE THIRD CENTURY.	
	Persecution under Septimius Severus.	
	The Rescript,	20
	Account by Tertullian,	20
	Account by Eusebius,	21
	Persecution under Maximinus Thrax.	
	Account by Eusebius,	21
	Lactantius on the death of Decius,	21
	Persecution under Valerian.	
	Cyprian's Letter,	22
	Martyrdom of Cyprian,	23
	Decree of Aurelian,	26
VII.	TRIUMPH OF CHRISTIANITY.	
	Edicts of Diocletian,	26
	Edict of Toleration by Galerus,	28
	Decree of Milan,	29
VIII.	SELECT BIBLIOGRAPHY,	31

I. INTRODUCTION.

The tradition of the ten persecutions of the Christians is of no value, for, if looked at in one way, the number is entirely too small, or, if it has reference only to the great persecutions, it is too large. Gibbon suggests that the ingenious parallels of the ten plagues of Egypt and the ten horns of the Apocalypse first suggested this calculation to the ecclesiastical writers of the fifth century, who determined this number. According to this calculation, the ten persecutions were those which occurred under Nero, Domitian, Trajan, Marcus Aurelius, Septimius Severus, Maximinus, Decius, Valerian, Aurelian, and Diocletian and Galerius.

There was no general persecution until after the decree of Decius (250 A.D.). Before this all persecutions were the results of administrative action, and consequently might occur at any time and at any place without affecting the rest of the empire. They depended on local feeling and the character of the governor, not on that of the emperor.

The Christians were outlaws and it was for the Name that they were persecuted, not because they held illegal assemblies: they were members of a body essentially hostile to the organization of the state. Nero originated the policy, when he seized upon the Christians as scapegoats to avert the suspicion which had fallen on him of having set fire to Rome; and this he probably made a permanent, systematic measure of administration.

After the time of Nero, persecutions of greater or less intensity and extent broke out now and then according to circumstances; but it is to be noted that they were always a possibility. When consulted, Trajan, Hadrian and Marcus Aurelius all indorsed this policy in rescripts to provincial governors: Christians were not to be sought out, but were to be condemned to death for the Name when an accusation was brought against them by a definite person.

The extract from Tertullian is noteworthy because he, in common with all the early church fathers, insisted that only bad emperors persecuted; modern scholars are wont to say that a good emperor, who had the welfare of the state at heart, was almost necessarily a persecutor. Tertullian's statement may have been biased, to some extent, by the fact that it was made in an apology, which was intended to influence official action.

TERTULLIAN'S GENERAL STATEMENT.

Liber Apologeticus, ch. 5, Opera ed. Oehler (Leipsic, 1853) vol. I, p. 130 sq. Latin.

To reconsider the origin of such laws, there was an old decree that no God should be consecrated by the emperor, unless sanctioned by the senate. M. Aemilius knows how it was with his god, Alburnus. And this is an argument for our cause that among you divinity is allotted at the caprice of man. Unless the god has won the favor of man, he is not a god; presently man will have to be propitious to the god.

Tiberius, therefore, in whose time the Christian name was made known to the world, sent to the senate, with the sanction of his favor, the information which he had received from Syrian Palestine which had revealed there the truth concerning the God himself. The senate, because it had not recommended the measure, rejected it. Cæsar kept his purpose and threatened those who accused the Christians. Consult your annals; there you will find that Nero was the first to rage with the imperial sword against this sect, then rising rapidly in Rome. But we even glory in such an author of our condemnation. For anyone who knows him cannot but see that nothing but what was pre-eminently good was condemned by Nero. And Domitian, a limb of Nero for cruelty, essayed persecution, but, because he was human too, he soon checked it and even restored those whom he had exiled. It is always such as these who are our persecutors, men unjust, impious and base; men whom you yourselves are not only accustomed to condemn, but whose victims you restore.

From the whole number of princes, wise in affairs divine and human, point out anyone, from that time up to the present day, hostile to the Christians. But we, on the other hand, show you a protector, if the letters of the most venerable emperor, M. Aurelius, are examined which testify that the prayers of the Christians, who happened to be soldiers, secured a shower which put an end to that drought in Germany. As he did not openly free this class of men from the penalty, yet by another method he did openly make it of no avail, for he added a condemnation for the informers, and that a more severe one.

What kind of laws are these which are enforced against us only by the impious, the unjust, the base, the savage, the false, and the mad; which Trajan frustrated in part by forbidding Christians to be sought out; which no Hadrian, although a man who pried into all novelties, no Vespasian, although a conqueror of the Jews, no Pius, no Verus ever executed? It would certainly be more readily thought that the worst would be eradicated by the best, by their enemies rather than by their friends.

II. PERSECUTION UNDER NERO.

This took place in 64 A. D. Tacitus' account is the best known and the most important. As a boy, he may have witnessed the fire and the persecution. An account of the fire immediately precedes the passage here quoted. There is not, as used to be supposed, any opposition between his account and that given by Suetonius. The latter says very little about the persecution, but it is interesting to see by the context how he regarded it.

The passage from Clement, which Ramsay and Lightfoot date about 97 A. D., probably refers chiefly to the Neronian persecution. But Ramsay says: (p. 310) "Clement is most naturally understood as referring to a continuous persecution throughout his own generation, keener, perhaps, at one time than at others."

For this persecution compare Eusebius, Book II, ch. 25; Orosius, Book VII, ch. 7. Juvenal, First Satire, verses 155 ff.; and Revelations, passim, are often cited.

Sulpicius Severus adds this bit quoted from him, after an account of the fire at Rome and the subsequent persecution of the Christians which he copied from Tacitus.

ACCOUNT BY TACITUS.

Annales XV, 44, ed. H. Furneaux, Oxford (1891) vol. III, p. 526. Latin.

Therefore to check this rumor, those, who were called Christians by the mob and hated for their moral enormities, were substituted in his place as culprits by Nero and afflicted with the most exquisite punishments. Christ, from whom the name was given, was put to death during the reign of Tiberius, by the procurator Pontius Pilate. Although checked for the time, this pernicious superstitution broke out again not only in Judea, where the evil originated, but throughout the City, in which the atrocities and shame from all parts of the world center and flourish. Therefore those who confessed were first seized, then on their information a great multitude were convicted, not so much of the crime of incendiarism, as of hatred of the human race. The victims who perished also suffered insults, for some were covered with the skins of wild beasts and torn to pieces by dogs, while others were fixed to crosses and burnt to light the night when daylight had failed. Nero had offered his gardens for the spectacle and was giving a circus show, mingling with the people in the dress of a driver, or speeding about in a chariot. Although they were criminals who deserved the most severe punishment, yet a feeling of pity arose since they were put to death not for the public good but to satisfy the rage of an individual.

ACCOUNT BY SUETONIUS.

Vita Neronis XVI, ed. Carl Roth, Leipsic, (1891) p. 176 sq. Latin.

In his reign many things were severely censured and suppressed and many also instituted: a limit was set to lavish expenditure; public dinners were reduced to doles; cook shops were forbidden to sell any prepared food except pulse or herbs, whereas formerly all kinds of relishes had been offered; Christians, a class of men of a new and vicious superstition, were subjected to severe punishments; the quadriga races were forbidden, because the charioteers wandered about, and by long license, assumed the right to make a jest of cheating and stealing; the partisans of the pantomimes were banished together with the actors themselves; to prevent forgery, means were first devised by which no document was to be sealed until it had been perforated and a thread run through three times.

ACCOUNT BY CLEMENT.

First Epistle to the Corinthians, ch. V, VI, VII. (Patres Apostoli, ed. Cotelerius, Antwerp, 1700.) Greek.

V. But to leave ancient examples, let us come to the recent champions, let us take the noble examples furnished by our own generation. On account of emulation and envy, those who were faithful and most righteous pillars of the church have suffered persecution even unto death.

Let us set before our eyes the holy Apostles. Peter by unjust envy endured not one or two, but many sufferings; and so, made a martyr, he departed to the peace of glory due him. On account of envy Paul obtained the reward of patience, after he had been seven times in bonds, and had been whipped and stoned. He preached in the East and in the West and received the glorious reward of his faith. He taught the whole world righteousness, and coming to the extreme West he suffered martyrdom under the governors, so that he departed from the world and went to his holy place, a great example of patience.

VI. Unto these men of holy lives were joined a vast multitude of the elect, who suffering much disgrace and many torments on account of envy, were a most noble example for us. On account of envy, women were tormented; Danaides and Dirce, when they suffered severe and unjust punishments, they persevered in their constant faith, and thou weak in body received a glorious reward. Envy has alienated women from their husbands and has changed that saying of our father Adam: "This is now bone of my bone and flesh of my flesh." Envy and strife have overturned great cities and rooted out great nations.

VII. These things, beloved, we write not only for your instruction, but also for your own remembrance; for we are in the same lists and the same contest is imposed upon us. . . . . .

ACCOUNT BY SULPICIUS SEVERUS.

Chron. II. 29, Opera ed. C. Halm, (1864). Corp. Script. Ecc. Lat. (Vienna), I. p. 88. Latin.

Then he began to rage against the Christians. Afterwards he even made laws forbidding the religion, and published edicts, ordering that Christianity should not exist. At this time Paul and Peter were condemned; one of them was beheaded. Peter was crucified.

III. PERSECUTION UNDER DOMITIAN.

There is no mention of a persecution during this reign, until the middle of the second century, and then we have only a few doubtful passages. Early traditions, however, strenuously affirm that Domitian was a persecutor and as Mommsen suggests, these few cases happen to have been recorded by profane writers because people of note were involved.

The bit from Sulpicius Severus is probably a reproduction of a lost passage of the Histories of Tacitus, and indicates the attitude of the Flavians to the Christians. Allard and Ramsay are both of this opinion.

Dio Cassius wrote in the second century, much later than the time of this persecution. His works are preserved only in the Epitome by Xiphilinus. He did not mention Christians by name, at all. This passage is the only one in which any pagan writer mentions that Domitian punished any one for religious reasons.

Suetonius' use of the phrase "contemptible indolence" has seemed to some scholars a proof that Clemens was a Christian. See Lightfoot and Ramsay especially.

THE FLAVIAN POLICY.

Sulpicius Severus, Chron. Lib. II, Ch. 30, ed. C. Halm (Corp. Script. Ecc. Lat. I. p. 90.) Latin.

It is reported that Titus previously summoned a council to deliberate as to whether a building of such wonderful workmanship as the Temple should be destroyed. Some thought that this sacred edifice, glorious beyond human construction, ought not to be destroyed, and that, if it were preserved it would furnish evidence of Roman moderation, but, if destroyed, it would be an everlasting proof of cruelty. On the other hand, others, and even Titus himself, were of the opinion that the Temple ought to be destroyed, particularly in order that the religions of the Jews and Christians should be completely rooted out, for granting that these religions are opposed to each other, yet they were both originated by the same authors. The Christians sprang from the Jews: the root being destroyed, the branch would soon perish. Thus the spirits of all were roused and by the will of God the Temple was destroyed three hundred and thirty-one years ago.

ACCOUNT BY DIO CASSIUS.

Histor. Rom. (excerpt. per Xiphilinum) Bk. LXVII, ch. 14. ed. Leipsic, 1829, Vol. IV. p. 97. Greek.

At this time [95 A. D.] the road leading from Sinuessa to Puteoli was paved with stones. And in the same year Domitian put to death, besides many others, his cousin Flavius Clemens, who was then consul, and the wife of Flavius, Flavia Domitilla, who was his own relative. The crime charged against both was sacrilege. On the same charge many others who had adopted Jewish customs were condemned. Some were put to death, others had their property confiscated. Domitilla was exiled alone on Pandataria.[1]

ACCOUNT BY SUETONIUS.

Vita Dom. XV, ed Carl Roth, Leipsic (1891) p. 250. Latin.

Finally, on the very slightest suspicion, he suddenly slew, before he was fairly out of his consulship his cousin, Flavius Clemens, a man of most contemptible indolence, whose sons, when mere children, he had

---

[1] Some scholars translate the next sentence in Dio Cassius as follows: "Domitian put to death Glabrio, who had been consul with Trajan, accused among other things of the same crimes." See Allard: Histoire I, 109. In order to show how faulty this translation is we give the Greek: Τὸν δὲ δὴ Γγαβρίωνα τὸν μετὰ τοῦ Τραιανοῦ ἄρξαντα κατηγορηθέντα τά τε ἄλλα καὶ οἷα οἱ πολλοὶ καὶ ὅτι καὶ θηρίοις ἐμάχετο, ἀπέκτεινεν.

publicly designated as his successors and had ordered, after having dropped their own names, the one to take the name Vespasian, and the other, Domitian.

IV. ATTITUDE OF TRAJAN AND HADRIAN.

Until recently it has been generally believed that this letter from Trajan to Pliny changed the legal status of the Christians. In spite of the uniform tradition of the early church that Trajan had favored them ("the laws which in part Trajan made void," Tertullian: Apology, Ch. V), scholars assumed that he first made the Name a sufficient cause for condemnation. This persecution took place in 112 or 113.

The rescript of Hadrian is appended to the first Apology of Justin Martyr, probably written 140 A. D. Formerly there was much doubt as to its authenticity, but Lightfoot, Mommsen, Ramsay, and Allard have added the weight of their authority in favor of its genuineness.

PLINY'S LETTER TO THE EMPEROR TRAJAN.

Epist. X, 96, 97, ed H. Keil, Leipsic (1870), p. 307 sq. Latin.

It is my custom, my lord, to refer to you all things concerning which I am in doubt. For who can better guide my indecision or enlighten my ignorance?

I have never taken part in the trials of Christians: hence I do not know for what crime or to what extent it is customary to punish or investigate. I have been in no little doubt as to whether any discrimination is made for age, or whether the treatment of the weakest does not differ from that of the stronger; whether pardon is granted in case of repentance, or whether he who has ever been a Christian gains nothing by having ceased to be one; whether the name itself without the proof of crimes, or the crimes, inseparably connected with the name, are punished. Meanwhile I have followed this procedure in the case of those who have been brought before me as Christians. I asked them whether they were Christians a second and a third time and with threats of punishment, I questioned those who confessed, I ordered those who were obstinate to be executed. For I did not doubt that, whatever it was that they confessed, their stubbornness and inflexible obstinacy ought certainly to be punished. There were others of similar madness, who because they were Roman citizens, I have noted for sending to the City. Soon, the crime spreading, as is usual when attention is called to it, more cases arose. An anonymous accusation, containing many names, was presented. Those who denied that they were or had been Christians, ought, I thought, to be dismissed since they repeated after me a prayer to the gods and made supplication with incense and wine to your image, which I had ordered to be brought for the purpose together with the statues of the gods, and since besides they cursed Christ, not one of which things they say, those who are really Christians can be compelled to do. Others, accused by the informer, said that they were Christians and afterwards denied it; in fact, they had been but had ceased to be, some many years ago, some even twenty years before. All both worshipped your image and the statues of the gods, and cursed Christ. They continued to maintain that this was the amount of their fault or error that, on a fixed day, they were accustomed to come together before daylight and to sing by turns a hymn to Christ as a god, and that they bound themselves by oath, not for some crime but that they would not commit robbery, theft, or adultery, that they would not betray a trust or deny a deposit when called upon. After this it was their custom to disperse and to come together again to partake of food, of an ordinary and harmless kind, however; even this they ceased to do after the publication of my edict in which according to your command I had forbidden associations. Hence I believed it the more necessary to examine two female slaves, who were called deaconesses, in order to find out what was true, and to do it by torture. I found nothing but a vicious, extravagant superstition. Consequently I postponed the examination and make haste to consult you. For it seemed to me that the subject would justify consultation, especially on account of the number of those in peril. For many of all ages, of every rank, and even of both sexes are and will be called into danger. The infection of this superstition has not only spread to the cities but even to the villages and country districts. It seems possible to stay it and bring about a reform. It is plain enough that the temples, which had been almost deserted, have begun to be frequented again, that the sacred rites, which had been neglected for a long time, have begun to be restored, and that fodder for victims, for which till now there was scarcely a purchaser, is sold. From which one may readily judge what a number of men can be reclaimed if repentance is permitted.

TRAJAN'S REPLY.

You have followed the correct procedure, my Secundus, in conducting the cases of those who were accused before you as Christians for no general rule can be laid down as a set form. They ought not to be sought out; if they are brought before you and convicted they ought to be punished; provided that he who denies that he is a Christian, and proves this by making supplication to our gods, however much he may have been under suspicion in the past, shall secure pardon on repentance. In the case of no crime should attention be paid to anonymous charges, for they afford a bad precedent and are not worthy of our age.

RESCRIPT OF HADRIAN TO MINUCIUS FUNDANUS.

Justin Martyr, Opera. ed. Otto, Jena (1842), I, p. 273 sq. Greek.

I have received the letter written to me by your predecessor, Serenus Granianus, a most excellent man: and it does not seem well to pass over this report in silence, lest both the innocent be confounded and an occasion for robbery be given to false accusers. Accordingly, if the inhabitants are able to sustain their accusations openly against Christians, so as to charge them with something before the tribunal, I do not forbid them to do this. But I do not permit mere tumultuous cries and acclamations to be used, for it is much more equitable that if anyone wishes to make accusation, you should know the charges. If, therefore, anyone charges and proves that the men designated have done anything contrary to the laws, you are to fix penalties in proportion to their transgressions. By Hercules, you will take especial care, that if, for the sake of calumny, anyone shall prosecute one of them, that you inflict on the accuser a more severe punishment for his villany.

V. PERSECUTION UNDER MARCUS AURELIUS.

Two points may well surprise us: first, that such a bitter persecution should have taken place under "the best of emperors;" and, secondly, that Tertullian, in spite of this persecution of which he probably knew, should have spoken of Marcus Aurelius as being favorably inclined towards the Christians. The first point may be explained in part by recalling that in the only passage of his Meditations, in which the emperor speaks of the Christians, he styles their attitude "sheer obstinacy."

The account of the persecution at Lyons and Vienna is especially valuable because it is from a letter written by eye-witnesses. It is a subject of regret that Eusebius did not preserve the whole letter. The date of the persecution was 177.

THE PERSECUTION AT LYONS AND VIENNA.

Eusebius: Historia Ecclesiastica, Book V, ch. I, 3 ff. (ed. Dindorf, Vol. IV, Leipsic, 1871, pp. 183-198). Greek.

"The servants of Christ, living at Vienna and Lyons in Gaul, to the brethren throughout Asia and Phrygia who have the same faith and hope of redemption that we have, peace, grace and glory from God the Father and Christ Jesus our Lord."

Then after some other preliminary remarks they begin their account in the following words: "The magnitude of the tribulation here, the great fury of the heathen against the saints, and how much the blessed martyrs endured, we cannot fully recount, nor indeed is it possible to express these in writing. For with all his might the adversary broke loose upon us, showing even now how unrestrained his future coming would be. He tried every means of training and exercising his followers against the servants of God, so that not only were we excluded from houses, baths and markets, but also forbidden, every one of us, to appear in any place whatsoever.

But the grace of God fought against the adversary, rescued the weak, and arrayed firm pillars, able through patience to withstand every attack of the Evil One. They engaged in conflict with him, suffering every kind of shame and injury, and, counting their great trials as small, they hastened to Christ, showing that 'the sufferings of this present time are not worthy to be compared with the glory which shall be revealed to us ward.'

First, indeed, they endured nobly the sufferings heaped upon them by the general populace, clamors, blows, being dragged along, robberies, stonings, imprisonments, and all that an enraged mob loves to inflict on opponents and enemies. Then they were taken to the forum by the chiliarch and the ordained authorities of the city and were examined in the presence of the whole multitude. Having confessed, they were imprisoned until the arrival of the governor. When they were afterwards brought before him and he treated us with all manner of cruelty, Vettius Epagathus, one of the brethren, filled with love for God and his neighbor, interfered. His daily life was so consistent that, although young, he had a reputation like the elder Zacharias, for he 'walked in all the commandments and ordinances of the Lord blameless' and was untiring in every good office for his neighbor, filled with zeal for God and fervent in spirit. Such a man could not endure the unrighteous judgment against us, but was filled with indignation and demanded that he should be permitted to testify in behalf of the brethren that there was no atheism or impiety in us. Those about the tribunal cried out against him, and with reason, for he was a man of mark, and the governor denied his just request, but asked only this one question, if he also was a Christian; and on his confessing this most distinctly, placed him also in the number of the martyrs. He was called the advocate of the Christians, but he had the Advocate [Παράκλητον] in himself, the Spirit more fully than Zacharias. This he manifested by the fulness of his love, counting himself happy to lay down his own life in the defence of the brethren. For he was and is a true disciple of Christ, 'following the Lamb whithersoever he goeth.'

After that the others were divided and the proto-martyrs were known and held in readiness. They with all eagerness finished the confession of martyrdom. But some appeared unprepared and untrained and still weak, unable to endure the strain of a great contest. Of these about ten became apostates, who caused us great pain and excessive sorrow, and weakened the zeal of the others who had not yet been seized, and who, although suffering all kinds of evil, were constantly with the martyrs and did not abandon them. Then indeed all were in great fear on account of the uncertainty of the confession, not fearing the sufferings to be endured, but looking to the end and fearing lest some one should apostatize. Yet those who were worthy were seized each day, filling up their number, so that all the zealous and those through whom especially our affairs had been managed were gathered together from the two churches. And some of our servants who were heathens were seized because the governor had ordered that we should all be examined in public.

These by the wiles of Satan, fearing the tortures which they saw the saints suffering and urged by the soldiers to do this, accused us falsely of Thyestean banquets and Oedipodean incests and of deeds which it is not lawful for us to speak of, or think of, and which we do not believe men ever committed. When these accusations were reported all raged like wild beasts against us, so that those even who had previously restrained themselves on account of kinship, then became exceedingly enraged and gnashed their teeth against us. And the saying of our Lord was fulfilled that 'the time will come when whosoever killeth you will think that he doeth God's service.' Then finally the holy martyrs endured sufferings beyond all description and Satan strove earnestly that some blasphemies might be uttered by them also.

But the whole rage of the people, governor and soldiers was aroused exceedingly against Sanctus, deacon from Vienna, and against Maturus, a recent convert but a noble combatant, and against Attalus, a native of Pergamus, who had always been a pillar and a foundation in that place, and against Blandina through whom Christ showed that what appears mean, deformed and contemptible to men is of great glory with God through love for Him, shown in power and not boasting in appearance. For while we all, together with her mistress on earth, who was herself also one of the combatants among the martyrs, feared lest in the strife she should be unable to make her confession on account of her bodily weakness, Blandina was filled with such power that she was delivered and raised above those who took turns in torturing her in every manner from dawn till evening; and they confessed that they were defeated and had nothing more which they could do to her. They marvelled at her endurance, for her whole body was mangled and broken; and they testified that one form of torture was sufficient to destroy life, to say nothing of so many and so great tortures. But the blessed one, like a noble athlete, renewed her strength in the confession; and her comfort, refreshment and relief from suffering was in saying, 'I am a Christian' and 'Nothing vile is done by us.'

Sanctus also himself, marvellously and beyond all men, endured nobly all human outrages, while the wicked hoped by the duration and severity of the tortures to wring from him something which he ought not to utter, he withstood them with such firmness, that he did not even tell his own name or the nation or the city whence he came, or whether he was a bondman or free, but to all questions he replied in the Roman tongue, 'I am a Christian.' This he confessed instead of name and city and race and everything else, and the people did not hear him utter another word. Then the governor and those who were torturing him became exceedingly obstinate against him, so that when they had nothing else that they could do to him, they at last applied red-hot brass plates to the most tender parts of his body. These indeed were burned, but he remained unsubdued and unshaken, firm in his confession, refreshed and strengthened by the celestial spring of the water of life flowing from the bowels of Christ. But his body was a witness of his sufferings, all one wound and scar, shriveled up and without human appearance externally. Christ, suffering in him, showed great wonders, defeating the adversary and exhibiting an example to tl others, that there is nothing fearful where the love of the Father exists, nothing painful where the glory of Christ is. For when the lawless men tortured the martyr again after some days, and thought that as his body was swollen and inflamed, if they applied the same tortures, they would overcome him, since he could not bear the touch of a hand; or that, if he died under the tortures, it would strike the others with terror, not only no such thing happened to him, but even contrary to all human expectations, his body arose and stood up straight during the remaining tortures and took on its former appearance and recovered the use of the limbs, so that through the grace of Christ the second torture was not suffering but healing.

But the devil, thinking he had already consumed a certain Biblias, one of those who had recanted, wishing also to condemn her on account of blasphemy, led her to the torture to compel her, as she was already feeble and weak, to utter impious things concerning us. But she recovered herself in her suffering, and, as if aroused from a deep sleep and reminded by the present anguish of the eternal torture in hell, she contradicted the blasphemers, saying: 'How could they eat children to whom it is not even lawful to taste the blood of irrational animals?' And after that she confessed herself a Christian and was placed in the order of the martyrs.

But as the tyrannical tortures were deprived of effect by Christ, through the patience of the blessed, the devil invented other contrivances, confinement in the dark and in the most loathsome place in the prison, stretching the feet in stocks extended to the fifth hole, and other torments such as attendants when enraged and filled with the devil are accustomed to inflict upon prisoners, so that very many were suffocated in prison who the Lord willed should depart thus, manifesting His glory. For some who had been tortured cruelly, so that it seemed impossible that they should live, even when every means was applied to heal them, remained in the prison, destitute of care from men, strengthened by the Lord and invigorated in body and soul, exhorting and encouraging the others. But the young and those recently arrested, whose bodies were not inured to torture, could not endure the severity of the imprisonment, but died in prison.

The blessed Pothinus, who had been entrusted with the office of bishop in Lyons, was dragged to the tribunal. He was over ninety years of age and very weak in body, breathing with difficulty on account of his physical weakness, but invigorated with spiritual zeal because of his intense eagerness for martyrdom. His body was worn out by old age and disease, but life was preserved in him in order that Christ might triumph in it. When he was carried by the soldiers to the tribunal and was accompanied by the magistrates of the city and the whole multitude who uttered all kinds of outcries against him, as if he were Christ Himself, he bore noble witness.

On being asked by the governor who was the god of the Christians, he said, 'If you are worthy you shall know.' Then he was dragged off harshly and endured many blows. Those near him struck him with their hands and feet in every manner, regardless of his age; those at a distance threw at him whatever they had in their hands; all thinking that they would sin extremely and be guilty of great impiety if any insult to him was omitted, for they thought thus to avenge their own gods. And scarcely breathing, he was cast into prison and died after two days.

Then indeed a certain great interposition of God occurred and the boundless mercy of Christ was shown in a manner that had rarely happened among the brotherhood, but not at all beyond the power of Christ. For those who had recanted when first arrested were imprisoned also and shared the sufferings. For their recantation was of no profit to them, even in this present time. But those who had confessed what they were, were imprisoned as Christians, no other charge being brought against them; but the former were treated as murderers and defiled with blood, and suffered twice as severely as the latter. For the joy of martyrdom and the hope of things promised and the love for Christ, and the Spirit of the Father encouraged the latter; but their consciences greatly terrified the former, so that their countenances were distinguishable from all the rest when they were led forth. For the former went forth joyfully, great glory and grace joining together in their countenances, so that their very bonds seemed to form beautiful ornaments for them, like those of a bride adorned with variegated golden fringes, and perfumed with the sweet fragrance of Christ, so that some thought them perfumed with earthly ointment. But the others were downcast, humble, sad, and filled with all kinds of disgrace, and in addition were reproached by the heathen as ignoble and cowardly, under the accusation of murder, and having lost all the honorable, glorious and life-giving Name. The others, when they saw this, were strengthened, and when arrested they confessed at once, paying no heed to the devil's suggestions."

After some other remarks they again continue: "Finally after t^h their martyrdom was divided into all kinds of forms. For plaitir crown of various colors and of all kinds of flowers they offered it to the Father. It was fitting indeed, that the noble athletes who had sustained a manifold conflict and had conquered grandly should obtain the great crown of immortality. Maturus, Sanctus, Blandina and Attalus were therefore led to the wild beasts in the amphitheatre, and in order to give to the heathen public a spectacle of cruelty, a day was especially appointed for our people to fight with the wild beasts. Accordingly Maturus and Sanctus again passed through the whole torture in the amphitheatre, not as if they had suffered nothing at all before, but rather as if having overcome the adversary already in many kinds of contests they were now striving for the crown itself. They endured again the running the gauntlet customary in that place and the attacks from the wild beasts and everything that the raging multitude, who cried out from one place or another, desired, and at last the iron chair in which their bodies were roasted and tormented them with the fumes. Not even with this did the tortures cease, but they raged still more, desiring to overcome their patience, and they did not hear a word from Sanctus except the confession which he had made from the beginning. These accordingly, after their life had continued for a very long time through the great conflict, died at last, after having furnished a spectacle to the world throughout that day instead of all the varieties of gladiatorial combats.

But Blandina suspended on a stake was exposed as food for the wild beasts which should fall upon her. Because she seemed to be suspended in the manner of a cross and because of her earnest prayers, she encouraged the contestants greatly. They looking upon her in her conflict, beheld with their eyes, through their sister, Him who had suffered for them in order to persuade those who trust in Him that everyone who suffers for the glory of Christ has eternal fellowship with the living God. And as none of the beasts touched her at that time, she was taken down from the stake and led away again to the prison, to be preserved for another contest, in order that, by conquering in more trials, she might make the condemnation of the crooked serpent irrevocable, and that she, small, weak and despicable, yet filled with Christ, the great and victorius Athlete, might encourage the brethren, and that she, after having overcome the antagonist in many contests, might obtain through the conflict the crown of immortality.

But when Attalus himself was loudly called for by the throng (for he was a distinguished man) he entered as a ready contestant on account of his good conscience, as he was truly skilled in the Christian discipline and had always been a witness of the truth among us. And as he was led about in the ring of the amphitheatre, a tablet was borne before him on which was written in the Roman, 'This is Attalus the Christian,' and the people were exceedingly indignant against him. But when the governor learned that this man was a Roman, he ordered him to be led away to prison again and to remain with the others who were there, concerning whom he had written to Caesar, from whom he was now awaiting an answer.

But the time which intervened was not wasted or profitless for them, for by their patience the boundless mercy of Christ was shown. For through the living the dead were restored to life and the witnesses showed favor to those who were not witnesses, and there was great joy for the virgin mother when she received back again living, those whom she had brought forth as dead. For through these the greater part of those who had been apostates retraced their steps, were again conceived, again endowed with life, and learned to confess. And now living and strengthened they went to the tribunal, while God, who desireth not the death of a sinner, but mercifully inviteth to repentance, regarded them kindly, in order that they might again be questioned by the governor. For Caesar had written that these should be put to death, but if any should deny they should be dismissed. At the beginning of the festival held there, which is attended by throngs of people from all nations, the governor had the blessed ones brought to the judgment-seat to be a show and spectacle for the multitude. Therefore he examined them again, and as many as seemed to be Roman citizens he had beheaded, the others he sent to the wild beasts.

Christ was glorified greatly in those who had previously denied him, for contrary to the expectation of the heathen, they confessed. For these were examined separately as about to be set free, and when they confessed, they were added to the number of the martyrs. But those who never had a particle of faith, or any expectation of the wedding garment, or any thought of the fear of God, remained without, and as sons of perdition blasphemed the way through their apostacy. All the others were added to the church. While these were examined a certain Alexander, a Phrygian by birth, and a physician by profession, who had resided in Gaul for many years, and who was extremely well-known to all by his love for God and boldness of speech, (for he was not without a share of apostolic grace) stood by the tribunal. By signs he encouraged them to confess and seemed to those who were standing about the tribunal as if he were in travail. But the multitude were enraged because those who had formerly apostatized now confessed, and cried out against Alexander as if he was the cause of this. / The governor stopped and asked him who he was; he replied that he was a Christian. Very angrily the governor condemned him to the wild beasts and on the following day he entered along with Attalus. For to please the mob the governor had again condemned Attalus to the wild beasts.

These having endured all the tortures which serve as punishments in the amphitheatre and having conquered in a great conflict, were finally put to death. Alexander did not groan or cry out at all, but communed in his heart with God. Attalus, when he was set in the iron chair and was burned so that the fumes from his body rose, said to the multitude, in the Roman tongue: "See this which ye do, is devouring men. But we do not devour men, or do anything else which is evil." When he was asked what name God has, he replied: "God does not have a name like a man."

After all of these, on the last day of the contests, Blandina was again brought in together with Ponticus, a boy of about fifteen. These had been brought every day to witness the sufferings of the others, and had been urged to swear by the idols. But as they had remained firm and had despised the idols, the multitude was furious against them, so that they had no compassion for the youth of the boy or the sex of the woman. But they subjected them to all the sufferings and led them through the whole round of torture, repeatedly urging them to swear, but not being able to accomplish this. For Ponticus, supported by his sister, so that even the heathen saw that she was encouraging and strengthening him, gave up his life after having nobly endured every torture. But the blessed Blandina last of all, like a noble mother having encouraged her children and having sent them before her victorious to the King, herself endured all the conflicts in which the children had suffered and hastened after them rejoicing and joyful in her departure, as if summoned to a marriage feast, rather than thrown to the wild beasts. After the scourgings, after the wild beasts, after the roasting, at last, enclosed in the net she was thrown before a wild bull. She was well tossed about by the animal, but she did not feel her sufferings on account of her hope, trust and communion with Christ, and at last she too died. And the heathen themselves confessed that no woman among

But not even thus was their madness and cruelty against the saints satisfied. For urged on by the wild beast, wild and barbarous tribes are not easily appeased, and their rage found another peculiar opportunity in the dead bodies. For the fact that they were conquered did not put them to shame, as they did not have any manly reason, but rather increased their wrath like that of a wild beast, and incited the hatred of the governor and people alike so that they treated us unjustly, that the Scripture might be fulfilled, 'He that is lawless, let him be lawless still, and he that is righteous, let him be righteous still.' For those who had been suffocated in the prison they threw to the dogs, carefully watching them night and day so that no one should be buried by us. And then they exposed the remnants left by the wild beasts and the fire, mangled and burnt. And the heads of the others together with their bodies, they likewise guarded unburied with soldiers for many days.

Some raged and gnashed their teeth against these, desiring to find some more severe vengeance against them. But others laughed and mocked at them, magnifying at the same time their own idols and imputing to the latter the punishment of the former. The more moderate, and those who had seemed to have some sympathy for them, reproached them frequently saying, 'Where is their God and what has their religion which they have preferred to their own lives, profited them?'

Such were the varied feelings among them, but we grieved greatly because we were not able to bury the bodies in the ground. For neither did night avail us for this purpose, nor bribes succeed, nor prayers move them. But they kept watch in every manner, as if it would profit them greatly if these were not buried."

After these they say in addition other things: "The bodies of the martyrs after having been exposed and exhibited in every manner for six days, were afterwards burned and reduced to ashes by the lawless men and thrown in the river Rhone which flows close by, so that no remnants of them might still be seen on the earth. And they did this as if they were able to overcome God and prevent their coming to life again, in order, as some said, 'that they may have no hope of a resurrection, trusting in which they bring to us a certain foreign and strange religion, and despise awful punishments and are ready with joy to suffer death. Now let us see whether they will rise again, and if their God is able to aid them and rescue them from our hands.'"

VI. PERSECUTIONS OF THE THIRD CENTURY.

The persecutions of the first half of the third century were merely local like those of the first two centuries, but in the second half they became general.

Several of the emperors of this first period were friendly to the Christians, and it is even said that Philip was a Christian; nevertheless persecutions took place, as the "Acta" of the martyrs prove. Septimius Severus tried to prevent pagans from becoming Christians by his rescript of 202, and Maximinus ordered the rulers of the churches to be put to death.

Although the text of the decree of Decius has not been preserved, we know that he promulgated a decree against the Christians, in 250 A. D., which instituted a general persecution. Of what the details were we can get some knowledge from the letters and documents of the time. The persecution may have been severe, but it was short, for Decius died in May, 251 A. D.

Decius attacked the whole body of the Christians, but Valerian adopted a different policy, since he condemned the heads of the community to death and seized the temporal possessions of the church. He issued two decrees, the second condemning bishops to death instead of merely to exile as the first did.

The so-called "Acta" are official draughts which were made in all civil and criminal cases, both at Rome and in the provinces, according to Roman law. Some of these reports of the trials of Christians are very valuable, but so many of them have been tampered with that they have to be used with caution.

The text of the decree by Aurelian has not been preserved in any official document, but the substance of it is probably given in the extract from the Passio Symphoriani.

PERSECUTION UNDER SEPTIMIUS SEVERUS.

THE RESCRIPT.

Spartian, Vita Sept. Sev. Ch. 17 (Script. Hist. August., ed. Jordan et Essenhardt I, p. 13). Latin.

Under threat of severe punishment he forbade men to become Jews. Moreover, he decreed the same in the case of Christians.

ACCOUNT BY TERTULLIAN.

Ad Scapulam, 4 (I, p. 547 sq. ed. Oehler). Latin.

Even Severus himself, father of Antoninus, was mindful of the Christians. For the Christian Proculus, who was called Torpacion, procurator of Euhodias, and who had once wrought a cure for him with ointment, Severus sought out and kept in his palace until the time of his death. Antoninus, who was nourished on Christian milk, was very well acquainted with this man. The most noble women and men whom Severus knew belonged to this sect, he not only did not harm, but he even set forth the truth by his own testimony and openly restored them to us from the raging populace.

ACCOUNT BY EUSEBIUS.

Hist. Ecc., Bk. VI, ch. 1. ed. Dindorf, Vol. IV, p. 239-40. Greek.

When Severus set in motion a persecution against the churches, brilliant testimonies were given everywhere by the athletes of religion. Especially did these abound in Alexandria, whither athletes of God were sent in accordance with their worth, from Egypt and all Thebais as if to a very great contest, and where they obtained their crowns from God through their most patient endurance of various tortures and kinds of death. Among these was Leonides, who was called the father of Origen, and who was beheaded, leaving his son still a young boy......

PERSECUTION UNDER MAXIMINUS THRAX.

ACCOUNT BY EUSEBIUS.

Hist. Ecc., Bk. VI, ch. 28. ed. Dindorf, Vol. IV; p. 273. Greek.

Maximinus Caesar succeeded to Alexander, emperor of the Romans, who had ruled thirteen years. On account of his hatred for the household of Alexander, which contained many believers, he began a persecution, but commanded that the rulers of the churches alone should be put to death, on the ground that they were the authors of the teaching of the Gospels. Then Origen composed his work "On Martyrdom," and dedicated the book to Ambrose and Protoctetus, who was presbyter of the parish in Caesarea, because both had incurred unusual peril in this persecution. The report is that in this peril these men were prominent in confession. Maximinus did not survive more than three years. Origen has marked this as the time of the persecution in the twenty-second book of his Commentaries on John and in different letters.

LACTANTIUS ON THE DEATH OF DECIUS.

De Mort. Persecut. ch. 4, Opera ed. O. F. Fritzsche (Bibl. Patr. Ecc. Lat. XI, Leipsic, 1844) II, p. 250 sq. Latin.

For after many years the accursed beast, Decius, arose who harrassed the church,—for who but an evil man can persecute righteousness?—And as if he had been raised to that high position for this pupose, he began at once to rage against God so that he immediately fell. For having proceeded against the Carpi, who had then occupied Dacia and Moesia, he was immediately surrounded by the barbarians and destroyed with a great part of his army. Nor could he be honored by burial, but, stripped and naked, he lay exposed as food to wild beasts and birds, as was becoming to an enemy of God.

PERSECUTION UNDER VALERIAN.

CYPRIAN'S LETTER.

Epist. 80, Opera ed. G. Hartel, II, p. 839 sq. (Corp. Script. Ecc. Lat. III, 1871.) Latin.

The reason why I did not write to you immediately, dearest brother, was that the whole body of the clergy were detained by the stress of the conflict, and could not depart thence at all, being prepared by the devotion of their spirits for everlasting and heavenly glory. Be it known to you that those have returned whom I had sent to the City to discover and report to us as to the nature of the truth of the rescript concerning us. For many, various and uncertain were the rumors circulated. But the truth of the matter is this: Valerian had sent a rescript to the senate, that bishops, presbyters and deacons should be punished immediately, but that senators, nobles, and Roman knights should be degraded from their dignity, and furthermore despoiled of their goods, and if, after they had been deprived of their property, they should persist in being Christians, they too should be beheaded. Matrons should be deprived of their goods and sent into exile. Those of Caesar's household, whoever had confessed formerly or should confess now, should have their property confiscated, and should be sent in chains by assignment to Caesar's estates. To his discourse, moreover, the emperor Valerian added a copy of the letter which he sent to the governors of the provinces concerning us. This letter we hope daily will arrive, prepared according to the strength of the faith, ready to endure martyrdom, and expecting by the might and grace of God the crown of eternal life. Be it known to you, moreover, that Xistus was executed in the cemetery on the eighth before the Ides of August, and together with him four deacons. Indeed, the prefects in the city insist daily on this persecution. If any are brought before them, they are punished and their goods confiscated to the treasury.

I beg that this may be made known through you to the rest of our associates, so that everywhere by their encouragement the brotherhood may be strengthened and prepared for the spiritual conflict, that each of us may not think more of death than of immortality, and that, consecrated to the Lord, in full faith and all virtue, they may rejoice rather than fear in this confession in which they know that, as soldiers of God and Christ, they will not be destroyed but be crowned. I hope that you, dearest brother, will be ever strong in the Lord.

THE MARTYRDOM OF CYPRIAN.

Acta Proconsularia Cypriani, Opera ed. G. Hartel, III, p. cx sqq. (Corp. Script. Eccles. Lat. III, 1871.) Latin.

In the fourth consulship of the emperor Valerian and the third of Gallienus, on the third before the Kalends of September, in the council chamber of Carthage, Paternus, the proconsul, said to Bishop Cyprian: "The most sacred emperors, Valerian and Gallienus have thought fit to give me a letter according to which they have ordered that those, who do not practice the Roman religion, should recognize the Roman rites. I have asked, therefore, concerning your name; what do you answer me?" Bishop Cyprian said: "I am a Christian and a bishop. I have known no other gods except the true and only God, who made heaven and earth, the sea and all that in them is. To this God we Christians yield ourselves; to Him we pray by day and night for you, for all men, and for the safety of the emperors themselves." Paternus, the proconsul, said: "Do you, then, persist in this purpose?" Bishop Cyprian replied: "A good purpose, which has known God, cannot be changed." Paternus, the proconsul, said: "Will you be able to depart into exile, then, to the city of Curubitana (Curubis) according to the decree of Valerian and Gallienus?" Bishop Cyprian said: "I depart." Paternus, the proconsul, said: "They have thought fit to write to me not only concerning bishops, but also presbyters. I wish, therefore, to learn from you who the presbyters are who abide in the city." Bishop Cyprian replied: "By your laws you have rightfully and profitably decreed that there should be no informers; and hence they cannot be betrayed and denounced by me. But in their own cities they will be found." Paternus, the proconsul, said: "To-day, in this place, I am going to seek them." Cyprian said: "Since custom forbids that any one offer himself voluntarily, and this is displeasing to your judgment, they cannot give themselves up, but, if you seek them, you will find them." Pate nus, the proconsul, said: "They will be found by me." And added: "It has also been ordered that they should not hold assemblies in any place or enter the cemeteries. If any one does not observe this so wholesome ordinance he is to be beheaded." Bishop Cyprian replied: "Do as you are ordered."

Then Paternus, the proconsul, ordered the blessed bishop Cyprian to be led into exile. When he had remained there for a long time, the proconsul Galerius Maximus succeeded the proconsul Aspasius Paternus and ordered the holy bishop Cyprian to be recalled from exile and brought before him. When the holy martyr Cyprian, chosen by God, had returned from the city of Curubitana, where he had been sent into exile by the order of Aspasius Paternus, the proconsul at that time, he remained in his gardens according to holy injunction, and thence daily hoped that it would happen to him as had been revealed. While he was waiting here, there suddenly came to him, on the Ides of September in the consulship of Tuscus and Bassus, two men of high rank, one the curator of the official Galerius Maximus, the proconsul, who had succeeded Aspasius Paternus, and the other the groom from the guards of this same official. And they put him between them, and brought him to Sexti, where Galerius Maximus, the proconsul, had retired for the sake of recovering his health. And so the proconsul Galerius Maximus ordered Cyprian to be reserved for him until the next day. And at the same time, the blessed Cyprian retired, led away to the chief and curator of this same official, Galerius Maximus, the proconsul, a most illustrious man, and he stayed with this man, enjoying his hospitality in the village, called Saturni, which is between Venerea and Salutaria. Thither the whole company of brethren came, and, when the holy Cyprian learned this, he ordered the maidens to be protected, since all had remained in the village before the gate of the hospitable officer.

And thus on the next day, the eighteenth before the Kalends of October, early in the morning, a great crowd came to Sexti according to the order of Galerius Maximus, the proconsul. And accordingly Galerius Maximus, the proconsul, ordered Cyprian to be brought before him that day, while he was sitting in the Sauciolian court. And when he had been brought, Galerius Maximus, the proconsul, said to bishop Cyprian: "You are Thascius Cyprian?" Bishop Cyprian replied: "I am." Galerius Maximus, the proconsul, said: "The most sacred emperors have commanded you to sacrifice." Bishop Cyprian said: "I will not." Galerius Maximus said: "Reflect on it." Bishop Cyprian replied: "Do what you are ordered to do. In such a just case there is no need of reflection."

Galerius Maximus, having spoken with the council, pronounced the sentence weakly and reluctantly in the following words: "For a long time you have lived in sacrilege, you have gathered about you many associates in your impious conspiracy, you have put yourself in hostility to the Roman gods and to the sacred rites, nor could the pious and most sacred princes, Valerian and Gallienus, emperors, and Valerian, the most noble Caesar, bring you back to the practice of their worship. And therefore, since you are found to be the author of the vilest crimes, and the standard bearer, you shall be a warning to those whom you have gathered about you in your crime; by your blood, discipline shall be established." And having said this he read out the decree from his tablet: "We command that Thascius Cyprian be executed by the sword." Bishop Cyprian said: "Thank God."

After this sentence the crowd of brethren kept saying: "And we will be beheaded with him." On account of this a commotion arose among the brethren and a great crowd followed him. And thus Cyprian was brought to the country about Sexti; here he laid aside his red cloak, kneeled on the ground, and prostrated himself before the Lord in prayer. And when he had laid aside his priestly robe and given it to the deacons, he stood in his linen under-garments,[1] and waited for the executioner. Moreover, when the executioner had come, he ordered his followers to give this executioner twenty-five pieces of gold. Indeed linen cloths and handkerchiefs were being sent before him by the brethren. After this the blessed Cyprian covered his eyes with his hand. When he could not bind the handkerchiefs to himself, Julian, the presbyter, and Julian, the subdeacon, bound them. Thus the blessed Cyprian died, and his body was placed near at hand on account of the curiosity of the heathen. Hence, being borne away in the night with tapers and torches, it was brought with prayers and great triumph to the courts of the procurator Macrobius Candidianus, which are on the Via Mappaliensis, near the fish ponds. Moreover, after a few days, Galerius Maximus, the proconsul, died.

The blessed martyr Cyprian suffered on the eighteenth before the

---

[1] Gibbon translates, he stood on a piece of linen (which the brethren ha' spread to catch his blood.)

Kalends of October under the emperors Valerian and Gallienus, Jesus Christ, the true God, reigning, to whom be honor and glory for ever and ever. Amen.

DECREE OF AURELIAN.

Passio S. Symphoriani Martyris, ch. 2 (Ruinart, Acta Martyrum Sincera, Amsterdam (1713) p. 80. Reprinted in Preuschen, Analecta.) Latin.

The emperor Aurelian to all his administrators and governors. We have learned that the precepts of the laws are violated by those who in our times call themselves Christians. Punish those who are arrested with divers tortures, unless they sacrifice to our gods, until the difficulty mentioned may be righted, and vengeance, satisfied by the extirpation of the crime, may have an end.

VII. THE TRIUMPH OF CHRISTIANITY.

This last persecution was the longest and the most severe. It covered approximately a period of ten years, which, however, was interrupted by civil wars, brought on by the establishment of the tetrarchy, and by the edict of toleration, granted by Galerius on his death bed. It was in Syria and Egypt that the persecution took its worst form. In the west the force of the decrees was mitigated, especially in the dominion of Constans.

We have two good authorities for the period, Eusebius and Lactantius, both contemporaries and eye-witnesses, the one in Phoenicia and Egypt, and the other in Nicomedia itself. From the two we get many details of the events leading up to the promulgation of the decrees, as well as of the horrors and cruelty attending their execution.

Eusebius says (Book VIII, 10) that the calamaties of the times were brought on the church as a judgment from God, since hypocrisy, rivalry and dissension had grown up in the church as a result of excessive liberty and great wealth.

Both in the case of the edict of toleration by Galerius and that by Constantine and Licinius, the original Latin text is to be found in Lactantius, and merely a Greek translation in Eusebius, (H. E., Bk. VIII, 17, and X, 5) Both Mason and Allard take this view. (For discussion of the authorship of the De mort. pers. see appendix to Vol. II of Gibbon, ed. by Bury, 1896.)

EDICTS OF DIOCLETIAN AGAINST THE CHRISTIANS.

Eusebius: Hist. Ecc., Book VIII, ch. 2, ch. 6 at end, and De Mart. Palest. ch. 3, ch. 4, and ch. 9. (ed. Dindorf, Vol. IV, p. 351, 357, 386, 390, 402.) Greek.

(Hist. Ecc. chap. 2.) This was the nineteenth year of the reign of

Diocletian, in Dystrus (which the Romans call March), when the feast of the Saviour's passion was near at hand, and royal edicts were published everywhere, commanding that the churches should be razed to the ground, the Scriptures destroyed by fire, those who held positions of honor degraded, and the household servants, if they persisted in the Christian profession, be deprived of their liberty.

And such was the first decree against us. But issuing other decrees not long after, the emperor commanded that all the rulers of the churches in every place should be first put in prison and afterwards compelled by every device to offer sacrifice.

(Hist. Ecc. chap. 6.) Then as the first decrees were followed by others commanding that those in prison should be set free, if they would offer sacrifice, but that those who refused should be tormented with countless tortures, who could again at that time count'the multitude of martyrs throughout each province, and especially throughout Africa and among the race of the Moors, in Thebais and throughout Egypt, from which having already gone into other cities and provinces, they became illustrious in their martyrdoms !

(De Mart. Pal. ch. 3.) During the second year the war against us increased greatly. Urbanus was then governor of the province and imperial edicts were first issued to him, in which it was commanded that all the people throughout the city should sacrifice and pour out libations to the idols. . . . .

(De Mart. Pal. ch. 4.) . . . . For in the second attack upon us by Maximinus, in the third year of the persecution against us, edicts of the tyrant were issued for the first time, that all the people should offer sacrifice and that the rulers of the city should see to this diligently and zealously.[1] Heralds went through the whole city of Caesarea, by the orders of the governor, summoning men, women and children to the temples of the idols, and in addition the chiliarchs were calling upon each one by name from a roll.

(De Mart. Pal. ch. 9.) . . . . All at once decrees of Maximinus again got abroad against us everywhere throughout the province. The governors, and in addition the military prefects, incited by edicts, letters and public ordinances the magistrates together with the generals, and the city clerks in all the cities, to fulfill the imperial edicts which

---

[1] Probably this was merely a republication of the edict given in the preceding extract.

commanded that the altars of the idols should be rebuilt with all zeal; and that all the men, together with the women and children, even the infants at the breast, should offer sacrifice and pour out libations; and these urged them anxiously, carefully to make the people taste of the sacrifices; and that the viands in the market should be polluted by the libations of the sacrifices; and that watches should be stationed before the baths, so as to defile those who washed in these with the all-abominable sacrifices. . . . .

EDICT OF TOLERATION BY GALERIUS. 311 A. D.

Lactantius, De Mort. Pers. ch. 34, 35. Opera ed. O. F. Fritzsche, II, p. 273. (Bibl. Patr. Ecc. Lat. XI. Leipsic, (1844.)

(Ch. 34.) Among other arrangements which we are always accustomed to make for the prosperity and welfare of the republic, we had desired formerly to bring all things into harmony with the ancient laws and public order of the Romans, and to provide that even the Christians who had left the religion of their fathers should come back to reason, since, indeed, the Christians themselves, for some reason had followed such a caprice and had fallen into such a folly that they would not obey the institutes of antiquity, which perchance their own ancestors had first established, but at their own will and pleasure, they would thus make laws unto themselves which they should observe and would collect various peoples in divers places in congregations. Finally, when our law had been promulgated to the effect that they should conform to the institutes of antiquity, many were subdued by the fear of danger, many even suffered death. And yet since most of them persevered in their determination, and we saw that they neither paid the reverence and awe due to the gods nor worshipped the God of the Christians, in view of our most mild clemency and the constant habit by which we are accustomed to grant indulgence to all, we thought that we ought to grant our most prompt indulgence also to these, so that they may again be Christians and may hold their conventicles, provided they do nothing contrary to good order. But we are going to notify the magistrates in another letter what they ought to do.

Wherefore, for this our indulgence, they ought to pray to their God for our safety, for that of the republic, and for their own, that the republic may continue uninjured on every side, and that they may be able to live securely in their homes.

(ch. 35). This edict is published at Nicomedia on the day before the Kalends of May, in our eighth consulship and the second of Maximinus.

DECREE OF MILAN (313 A. D.)

Lactantius, De Mort. Pers., ch. 48, Opera ed. O. F. Fritzsche, II, p. 288 sq. (Bibl. Patr. Ecc. Lat. XI, Leipsic, 1844). Latin.

When I, Constantine Augustus, as well as I, Licinius Augustus, had fortunately met near Mediolanum (Milan), and were considering everything that pertained to the public welfare and security, we thought that among other things which we saw would be for the good of many, that those regulations pertaining to the reverence of the Divinity ought certainly to be made first, so that we might grant to the Christians and to all others full authority to observe that religion which each preferred; whence any Divinity whatsoever in the seat of the heavens may be propitious and kindly disposed to us, and all who are placed under our rule. And thus by this wholesome counsel and most upright provision, we thought to arrange that no one whatever should be denied the opportunity to give his heart to the observance of the Christian religion or of that religion which he should think best for himself, so that the supreme Deity, to whose worship we freely yield our hearts, may show in all things his usual favor and benevolence. Therefore, your Worship should know that it has pleased us to remove all conditions whatsoever, which were in the rescripts formerly given to you officially, concerning the Christians, and now any one of these who wishes to observe the Christian religion may do so freely and openly, without any disturbance or molestation. We thought it fit to commend these things most fully to your care that you may know that we have given to those Christians free and unrestricted opportunity of religious worship. When you see that this has been granted to them by us, your Worship will know that we have also conceded to other religions the right of open and free observance of their worship for the sake of the peace of our times, that each one may have the free opportunity to worship as he pleases; this regulation is made that we may not seem to detract aught from any dignity or any religion. Moreover, in the case of the Christians especially, we esteemed it best to order that if it happens that anyone heretofore has bought from our treasury or from anyone whatsoever, those places where they were previously accustomed to assemble, concerning which a certain decree had been made and a letter sent to you officia' the same shall be restored to the Christians without payment or any claim of recompense and without any kind of fraud or deception. Those, moreover, who have obtained the same by gift, are likewise to return them at once to the Christians. Besides, both those who have purchased and those who have secured them by gift, are to appeal to the vicar if they seek any recompense from our bounty, that they may be cared for through our clemency. All this property ought to be delivered at once to the community of the Christians through your intercession, and without delay. And since these Christians are known to have possessed not only those places in which they were accustomed to assemble, but also other property, namely the churches, belonging to them as a corporation and not as individuals, all these things which we have included under the above law, you will order to be restored, without any hesitation or controversy at all, to these Christians, that is to say to the corporations and their conventicles:— providing, of course, that the above arrangements be followed so that those who return the same without payment, as we have said, may hope for an indemnity from our bounty. In all these circumstances you ought to tender your most efficacious intervention to the community of the Christians, that our command may be carried into effect as quickly as possible, whereby, moreover, through our clemency, public order may be secured. Let this be done so that, as we have said above, Divine favor towards us which, under the most important circumstances we have already experienced, may, for all time, preserve and prosper our successes together with the good of the state. Moreover, in order that the statement of this decree of our good will may come to the notice of all, this rescript, published by your decree, shall be announced everywhere and brought to the knowledge of all, so that the decree of this, our benevolence, cannot be concealed.

VIII. SELECT BIBLIOGRAPHY.

Allard: Histoire des Persécutions. 5 Vols. Paris, 1884-1894. (Second editions of Vols. I and II, Paris, 1892-1894.)
These volumes form the most important work on the whole period.

Allard: Le Christianisme et l'Empire Romain. 1 Vol. Paris, 1897.
This is a brief and more popular statement of the conclusions reached by this author in the preparation of his larger work. It is useful to the student because it contains a valuable bibliography of original sources and secondary works. The price is only three francs and fifty centimes.

Aubé: Histoire des Persécutions de l'Église. Paris, 1875-1885.
This work, although often quoted, is less scholarly than the preceding and has been superseded by more recent works.

Friedländer: Sittengeschichte Darstellungen aus der Roms. 3 Vols. Leipsic, 1888-1890.
This work is a valuable portrayal of the habits and daily life of the Romans. It should be studied in order to understand to what extent the Christians deviated from the customs of their fellow-citizens and why they antagonized the government.

Gibbon: Decline and Fall of the Roman Empire. Ed. Bury, Vols. I-III, London and New York, 1896-1897.
Gibbon's "impartial" account in the "infamous" fifteenth and sixteenth chapters is the most famous discussion of this subject in English. Anyone, who wishes to get an epitome of the history of the course of thought concerning this subject during the last century can do so by consulting Milman's and Smith's editions with the notes. Bury's edition, the most scholarly of all, omits all criticisms of Gibbon's attitude, and merely corrects mistakes as to matters of fact.

Hardy: Christianity and the Roman Government. London, 1894.
A brief and scholarly discussion of the early persecutions. It covers practically the same period as Ramsay's book and was written partly as a criticism of the latter.

Lightfoot: Saint Clement of Rome. London, 1870.
In this and in his other works, on "Saints Ignatius and Polycarp" and "The Apostolic Fathers," Lightfoot gives most scholarly and exhaustive discussions of each question treated by him. His bibliographical references and citations of authorities, "pro and con," are extremely full.

Mason: Persecution of Diocletian. Cambridge, 1876.
Popular, but useful, because in English.

Mommsen: Der Religions frevel nach römischen Recht, in the Historische Zeitschrift. Vol. LXIV, 1890, p. 389-424.

Among the many contributions by Mommsen to the study of early church history, this is possibly the most valuable. By his profound knowledge of Roman history and law, he disproved many theories currently held, and laid the foundation on which Ramsay, Hardy, and others have built.

Preuschen: Analecta, Frieburg and Leipsic. 1893.

This is a collection of short, original documents, illustrating the history of the early church. Most of the documents in this pamphlet, as well as many others, are given in the collection in the original text. The editing is carefully done and a good bibliography is given for each section.

Ramsay: The Church in the Roman Empire before 170 A. D. London, 1894.

A very careful and scholarly discussion. Original in treatment, although based upon Mommsen's articles. The notes furnish excellent bibliographical references to the work of other scholars, such as Overbeck, Arnold, Neumann, Lightfoot and others.

Renan: Les Origines du Christianisme. 6 Vols, Paris, 1863-1882.

By far the most exhaustive discussion of the period to the death of Marcus Aurelius. Every scrap of evidence available for the author was gathered and laid under contribution. His views may not be accepted, but his work is invaluable as a store-house of material.

The editors have consulted such translations as were accessible. In particular, indebtedness must be acknowledged to the series of "Nicene and Post-Nicene Fathers" for suggestions as to doubtful passages from Eusebius.

SERIES FOR 1894.

I. Early Reformation Period in England.* Single number, 20 pages.
II. Urban and the Crusaders.* Single number, 24 pages.
III. The Reaction after 1815.* Single number, 24 pages.
IV. Letters of the Crusaders.* Double number, 40 pages.
V. The French Revolution, 1789-1791.* Double number, 36 pages.
VI. English Constitutional Documents. Double number, 38 pages.

SERIES FOR 1895.

I. English Towns and Gilds. Double number, 40 pages.
II. Napoleon and Europe. Double number, 32 pages.
III. The Mediaeval Student. Single number, 20 pages.
IV. Monastic Tales of the XIII Century. Single number, 20 pages.
V. England in the Time of Wyclifle. Single number, 20 pages.
VI. Period of Early Reformation in Germany. Double number, 32 pages.
VII. Life of St. Columban. Double number, 36 pages.

SERIES FOR 1896.

I. The Fourth Crusade. Single number, 20 pages.
II. Statistical Documents of the Middle Ages. Single number, 23 pages.
III. Period of the Later Reformation. Double number, 32 pages.
IV. The Witch-Persecutions. Double number, July, 1897.
V. English Manorial Documents. Double number, 32 pages.
VI. The Pre-Reformation Period. Double number, 34 pages.

SERIES FOR 1897.

I. The Early Christian Persecutions. Double number, 32 pages.
II. Canons and Creeds of the First Four Councils. Double number, Sept.
III. Documents Illustrative of Feudalism. Double number, October.
IV. Ordeals, Compurgation, Excommunication, and Interdict. Double number, November.
V. Typical Cahiers of 1789. Double number, December.

Annual subscription, $1.00.
Single numbers, Vol. I, 15 cents; Vols. II, III and IV, 10 cents.
Double numbers, Vol. I, 25 cents; Vols. II, III and IV, 20 cents.
Bound Volumes, $1.50.
Discounts will be given on orders for 25 or more numbers.
Subscriptions and orders should be sent to

DANA C. MUNRO,

UNIVERSITY OF PENNSYLVANIA,

June, 1897.   Philadelphia, Pa.

---

* Revised edition.

Vol. IV.

Translations and Reprints

FROM THE

Original Sources of European History

THE CANONS

OF THE

FIRST FOUR GENERAL COUNCILS:

NICAEA, CONSTANTINOPLE, EPHESUS AND CHALCEDON.

EDITED BY EDWIN KNOX MITCHELL, D.D.

(Hartford Theological Seminary)

PUBLISHED BY

The Department of History of the University of Pennsylvania.

Philadelphia, Pa., 1898.

ENGLISH AGENCY: P. S. KING & SON, 12-14 King Street, London, S. W.

THE use by readers and students of those original documents from which our knowledge of history is so largely drawn has come to be valued in recent times at something like its true worth. The sequence of past events, the form and spirit of institutions, the characters of men, the prevailing habits of thought, obtain their greatest reality when we study them in the very words used by the men to whom the past was the living present. Even historians who have not been characterized by a close dependence on the results of patient investigation of the sources have recognized the superiority of an appeal to original testimony. Mr. Froude says, "Whenever possible, let us not be told about this man or that. Let us hear the man himself speak, let us see him act, and let us be left to form our own opinion about him." And in "Stones of Venice," Mr. Ruskin writes, "the only history worth reading is that written at the time of which it treats, the history of what was done and seen, heard out of the mouths of the men who did and saw. One fresh draught of such history is worth more than a thousand volumes of abstracts, and reasonings, and suppositions and theories."

Experience has proved, not only that the interest of students can be more readily obtained through the vividness of a direct and first-hand presentation, and that knowledge thus gained is more tangible and exact; but that the critical judgment is developed in no slight degree, and the ability as well as the interest for further study thus secured.

The utilization of the original sources of history has, however, been much restricted by their comparative inaccessibility. A great proportion of such documents as illustrate European history exist only in more or less unfamiliar languages; many are to be found only in large and expensive collections, or in works that are out of print and therefore difficult to obtain or consult.

The desire to overcome in some degree this inaccessibility, especially for their own classes, led the editors of the present series of translations and reprints from the original sources of European history to undertake its publication. During the past four years evidence has been given of the usefulness of the documents in several directions. Their most considerable use has naturally been with college classes. One or more of the issues has been used in twenty-five of the principal Universities and Colleges, and four Divinity Schools. In addition to these and their use in lower schools they have been found to give increased value to University Extension courses and reading circles.

During the current year the series will take on a somewhat different character. Instead of five or more numbers of 32 pages, there will be issued two numbers, each of about 100 pages. The first of these, which will be ready in May, will be edited by William Fairley, Ph. D., of the University of Pennsylvania. The remaining number, edited by James Harvey Robinson, of Columbia University, will appear in November. Titles of the numbers and further particulars are given on the third cover page.

Translations and Reprints

FROM THE

ORIGINAL SOURCES OF EUROPEAN HISTORY.

VOL. IV.   CANONS AND CREEDS OF THE FIRST FOUR GENERAL   No. 2
            COUNCILS.

TABLE OF CONTENTS.

		PAGE
I.	THE CREED AND CANONS OF NICÆA.	
	1. The Nicene Creed, ...	3
	2. Subjects of the Canons, ...	4
	3. Canons, ...	4
II.	THE CREED AND CANONS OF CONSTANTINOPLE.	
	1. The Creed, ...	11
	2. Subjects of the Canons, ...	12
	3. Canons, ...	12
III.	THE CANONS OF EPHESUS.	
	1. Subjects of the Canons, ...	15
	2. Canons, ...	15
IV.	DEFINITION OF FAITH AND CANONS OF CHALCEDON.	
	1. Definition of Faith,'	18
	2. Subjects of the Canons, ...	21
	3. Canons, ...	22
V.	SOURCES AND LITERATURE, ...	31

INTRODUCTION.

1. The Council of Nicæa was called by the emperor Constantine in the summer of A. D. 325, primarily for the settlement of the Arian controversy, which had greatly distracted the church; but also to deal with the Meletian schism in Egypt, and with the question as to the method of calculating the date for Easter. The titles and subject matter of its twenty Canons indicate, however, that there were many and diverse points brought before the Council for decision. There were some 318 bishops present, 7 of whom were Latins.

2. The Council of Constantinople was summoned by the Emperor Theodosius I, in May, A. D. 381, in order to reaffirm the Nicene faith and to secure it against Arianism and Macedonianism [Semi-Arianism], as well as to stay the progress of Apollinarianism, and to settle the dissensions in the church at Constantinople. There were 150 bishops present, none of whom were from the west.

3. The Council of Ephesus was called by Theodosius II, in June, A. D. 431, for the purpose of settling the Nestorian controversy, and of condemning Pelagianism. There were some 200 bishops present, 2 of whom were Latins.

4. The Council of Chalcedon was convoked by the emperor Marcian in October, A. D. 451; in order to denounce and nullify the action of the so-called Robbers' Synod which had met at Ephesus two years previous. There were some 600 bishops present, only 4 of whom were Latins.

[The following translation of the Canons is based upon the text of Dr. William Bright, and acknowledgment is hereby made of the assistance derived from his excellent notes, as well as from the English translation of Hefele by Clark and Oxenham.]

I. THE CREED AND CANONS OF THE FIRST GENERAL COUNCIL, HELD AT NICÆA, A. D., 325.

1. THE NICENE CREED AS FRAMED IN 325, ACCORDING TO THE TEXT CONTAINED IN THE ACTS OF THE COUNCIL OF CHALCEDON.

We believe in one God, the FATHER Almighty, Maker of all things visible and invisible. And in one Lord, JESUS CHRIST, the Son of God, begotten of the Father, the only-begotten; that is, of the essence of the Father, God of God, Light of Light, very God of very God, begotten, not made, being of one substance [$ὁμοούσιον$] with the Father; by whom all things were made, both in heaven and on earth; who for us men, and for our salvation, came down and was incarnate and was made man; he suffered, and the third day he rose again, ascended into heaven; from thence he shall come to judge the quick and the dead, And in the HOLY GHOST. But those who say: 'There was a time when he was not;' and 'He was not before he was made;' and 'He was made out of nothing,' or 'He is of another substance' or 'essence,' or 'The Son of God is created,' or 'changeable,' or 'alterable'—they are condemned by the holy catholic and apostolic church.

2. SUBJECTS OF THE CANONS.

1. Self-mutilation incompatible with clerical office.
2. Converts not to be ordained immediately after baptism.
3. 'Sub-introduced' women not to dwell with clerics.
4. On appointments to bishoprics in the provinces,
5. On excommunication, and on provincial synods.
6. All sees to retain their ancient rights. Bishops to be appointed according to rule.
7. Honorary precedence for the bishop of Aelia [Jerusalem].
8. On the treatment of converts from Novatianism.
9. On inquiry into character of ordinands.
10. Against ordaining those who have lapsed.
11. Laymen who lapsed without excuse to be put under penance.
12. On the case of those who resigned public office, but sought to regain it.
13. Communion to be given to all dying persons, including those under penance.
14. On lapsed catechumens.
15. Against migration of bishops and clergy.
16. Against clerics who leave their proper posts.
17. Against clerics who take usury.
18. Deacons not to encroach on privileges of presbyters.
19. On the treatment of converts from Paulianism.
20. Prayer to be offered standing on Sundays and throughout the Paschal season.

3. CANONS OF THE COUNCIL OF NICÆA.

CANON I. *Self-mutilation incompatible with clerical office.*

If any man has been operated upon by physicians during illness, or has been castrated by barbarians, he may remain among the clergy; but if a man in good health has castrated himself, he must withdraw, even though he is registered among the clergy; and from this time on, no one who has thus acted should be promoted. And clear as it is, that what has been said refers to those who have intentionally acted thus and have dared to castrate themselves, it is equally clear that the rule of discipline admits to the ranks of the clergy those who have been made eunuchs by barbarians or by their masters, provided they are in other respects found worthy.

CANON 2. *Converts not to be ordained immediately after baptism.*

Inasmuch as many things, either from necessity, or by reason of the pressure of certain persons, have happened contrary to the rule of the church, so that men who have just turned from a heathen life to the faith, and have spent but a short time as catechumens, are brought directly to the spiritual laver, and at baptism are exalted at once to the episcopate or presbyterate, it has seemed best that hereafter this should not take place. For [before being appointed to office] a man should spend considerable time as a catechumen, and should be tested farther after baptism; for the apostolic word is plain, which says: "Not a novice, lest, being puffed up, he fall into condemnation and the snare of the devil." If then, as time goes on, some grave, unspiritual fault be found in the person [thus hastily ordained], and this shall be established by two or three witnesses, he must resign his clerical office. Now any one who acts contrary to this ordinance, thus venturing opposition to the great Synod, will run a risk as to his clerical position.

CANON 3. *'Sub-introduced' women not to dwell with clerics.*

The great Synod has universally denied permission to either bishop, or presbyter or deacon, or any one at all in the clergy, to have an intimate female house companion, except it be a mother, or a sister, or an aunt, or such other woman as has escaped all suspicion.

CANON 4. *On appointments to bishoprics in the provinces.*

It is especially fitting that a bishop be appointed by all the bishops in the province; but if such a thing be difficult, owing either to urgent necessity, or to the distance, then three at least should come together, the absent bishops giving their votes and expressing their concurrence by letter; this done, the consecration should be performed. The ratification of such procedure, however, is in every province to be left to the metropolitan.

CANON 5. *On excommunication, and on provincial synods.*

As regards those who, whether in the rank of the clergy or among the laity, have been excommunicated by the bishops in this or that province, the sentence must hold good in accordance with the rule which prescribes that those who have been cast out by some bishops should not be admitted by others. However, let inquiry be made, whether such have not been unchurched through pettiness, or contentiousness, or some unkindliness of that sort on the part of the bishop. In order, therefore, that the matter may receive due examination, it has seemed good that there should be two synods every year in each province, that, by the gathering of all the bishops of a province into one assembly, such questions may be examined into, and thus that those who have undeniably offended against their bishop may appear to all to be with good reason excommunicate, until it may seem fitting to the common body of bishops to cast a milder vote in their behalf. And let the synods be held, one before Lent [Tessaracosta], that, all pettiness of soul being banished, the gift [of the eucharist] may be offered with a pure heart unto God; and the second some time late in the autumn.

CANON 6. All sees to retain their ancient rights. Bishops to be appointed according to rule.

Let the ancient customs prevail which obtain in Egypt and Libya and Pentapolis, and which give the bishop of Alexandria jurisdiction over all these provinces, since there is a similar custom in the case of the bishop of Rome. And likewise also at Antioch, and in the other provinces, their prerogatives are to be preserved to the churches. Now it is perfectly plain that if any one has become a bishop without the consent of the metropolitan, the great Synod has decreed that such a one ought not to remain a bishop. If, however, two or three, through their own contentiousness, antagonize the common vote of all the bishops, the same being reasonable and in accordance with church rule, the vote of the majority must prevail.

CANON 7. Honorary precedence for the bishop of Aelia (Jerusalem).

Since custom and ancient tradition have brought it about that the bishop in Aelia [Jerusalem] is specially honored, he may retain the position of honor, the proper dignity of the metropolis [Cæsarea] being, however, duly conserved.

CANON 8. On the treatment of converts from Novatianism.

With respect to those who at one time style themselves "the Pure" [i. e. Novatians], but afterward seek admission to the catholic and apostolic church, the holy and great Synod has seen fit to decree that they may remain in the clerical office, provided that they receive imposition of hands. But, first of all, they must make confession in writing that they will agree to the decrees of the catholic and apostolic church, and follow them: that is, by having fellowship with those who have married a second time, and also with those who have lapsed in persecution, if the church has appointed for such a season of penance and a definite time when they can return to fellowship. They will thus give evidence that they will follow all the decrees of the catholic church. Wherever, then, either in villages or cities, those who have received ordination shall be found to be entirely confined to their sect, the men thus found in the clerical office shall retain the same status as before. But if certain [Novatian] clerics seek admission to the catholic church when it already has a bishop or presbyter of its own appointment, it is plain that the bishop of the church shall retain the dignity of "bishop," while he who is styled "bishop" by the so-called "Pure," shall have the rank of presbyter: this, at least, unless the bishop be pleased to grant him a share in the honorary title of "bishop;" if he is not so minded, he should certainly find a place for him as rural bishop or presbyter, that he may seem to retain fully his clerical status. This provision, then, is made to prevent the anomaly of two ruling bishops in one city.

CANON 9. On inquiry into character of ordinands.

If any have been admitted as presbyters without due investigation, or if any, upon examination, have confessed to sins committed by them, and yet have received ordination by men who were moved by their confession, the rule does not accept them; for only a character above reproach will the catholic church defend.

CANON 10. Against ordaining those who have lapsed.

If any from the number of the lapsed have been chosen to office either in ignorance, or with the ordainer's full knowledge, this cannot prejudice the church's rule; for when their disqualification is discovered, they must be deposed.

CANON 11. Laymen who lapsed without excuse to be put under penance.

Regarding those who have fallen away, yet not under compulsion, nor for fear of confiscation of property or personal risk or the like (in other words, under conditions such as characterized the tyranny of Licinius), the Synod has decided to extend clemency to them, even though they are unworthy of kindly consideration. All those, therefore, who truly repent, if they were formerly among the "faithful," shall spend three years of penitence as "hearers," for seven years they shall be "kneelers," and for two they shall join with the people in the prayers, without, however, participating in the "oblation" [the eucharist].

CANON 12. On the case of those who resigned public office, but sought to regain it.

Those soldiers who were called by grace, and showed real zeal at the start, and threw away their belts, but who afterward returned like dogs to their own vomit, so that some even offered money, and secured reenlistment by bribes; these men must be "kneelers" ten years, even after having spent three years as "hearers." In the case of all such, there should be a thorough examination of their purpose, and of the nature of their repentance; for those who, by their reverence and tears and patience and good works, show their conversion in deed and not merely in appearance, may reasonably join in the prayers at the expiration of the time which it was appointed that they should spend as "hearers"; indeed the bishop may show even greater leniency toward them, if he deems it wise. But those who carry their penance all too lightly, and consider the mere form of entering the church a sufficient sign of their repentance, must by all means complete the full period.

CANON 13. Communion to be given to all dying persons, including those under penance.

With regard to those penitents who are departing this life, the old and regular law is still to be observed: viz. that if any one is departing, he should not be deprived of the last and most necessary provision for the journey. But if, after one's life has been despaired of, and he has partaken of the communion, he is again restored to the number of the living, he shall be in the class of those who join in the prayer only.

And, in general, if any one whatsoever is departing, and begs to partake of the eucharist, the bishop, after due examination of his fitness, shall present to him the "oblation."

Canon 14. On lapsed catechumens.

Respecting lapsed catechumens, the holy and great Synod has decided that for three years they shall be simply "hearers," and that thereafter they may pray with the catechumens.

Canon 15. Against migration of bishops and clergy.

Owing to the great disturbance and the many factions that have resulted from a custom, which, though contrary to rule, has been found prevalent in certain quarters, it has seemed best to entirely suppress it, and to ordain that neither bishop, nor presbyter, nor deacon obtain any transfer from city to city; and if, after the decision of the holy and great Synod, any cleric makes any such attempt, or devotes himself to such an enterprise, the arrangement shall be completely nullified, and he shall be restored to the church in which he was ordained bishop or presbyter.

Canon 16. Against clerics who leave their proper posts.

All those who recklessly withdraw from their church, neither having the fear of God before their eyes, nor taking pains to know the church's rules, whether they be presbyters, or deacons, or registered in any clerical office whatsoever, must by no means be received into another church, but the utmost pressure should be brought to bear upon them to induce them to return to their own diocese; or if they are bent upon staying, fellowship should be denied to them. And if any bishop has the temerity to underhandedly steal a cleric belonging to another bishop, and to ordain him in his own church, without the consent of the bishop from whom the registered cleric withdrew, the ordination shall be void.

Canon 17. Against clerics who take usury.

Inasmuch as many registered among the clergy, in covetous pursuit of sordid gain, have forgotten the divine Scripture which says: "He put not his money out at interest" [Ps. 14: 5 LXX.,] and when they make loans, demand 1 per cent. a month; the holy and great Synod has deemed it just to decree that if, after the publication of this ordinance, any one is found taking interest by explicit contract, or seeking to accomplish the same result in another way, or exacting half as much again when the debt falls due, or, in fine, resorting to any other contrivance whatsoever for the sake of base gain, he shall be deposed from the clerical office, and his name erased from the canon.

CANON 18. Deacons not to encroach on privileges of presbyters.

It has come to the knowledge of the holy and great Synod, that in certain regions and cities the deacons give the eucharist to the presbyters, although neither rule nor custom allows those, who have no authority to make the "oblation," to give the body of Christ to those who have such authority. And this also has come to light, that, in addition, some of the deacons partake of the eucharist before the bishops. All these abuses, then, must cease. And let the deacons remain in their proper sphere, remembering that they are merely the assistants of the bishop, and of lower rank than the presbyters. As is consistent, then with good order, let them receive the eucharist after the presbyters, at the hands of either the bishop or the presbyter. But let no deacon sit in the midst of the presbyters, for such a thing is contrary both to rule and good order. But if any one refuses to obey, even after hearing these ordinances, let him be removed from the diaconate.

CANON 19. On the treatment of converts from Paulianism.

With regard to those who have Paulianized [i. e. followed the heresy of Paul of Samosata], but who later have fled for refuge to the catholic church, the ordinance prescribes that they shall be rebaptized without exception; and if some, in time past, were registered among the clergy, they shall be ordained (after rebaptism) by the bishop of the catholic church, provided they approve themselves to be blameless and above reproach; if, however, the examination finds them unfit for the office, they should be deposed. This rule is to be observed, in like manner, with regard to deaconesses, and, in short, with all those registered among the clergy. We called special attention to the deaconesses, who have apparent clerical rank, since they have no real ordination, and are therefore to be reckoned as altogether of the laity.

CANON 20. Prayer to be offered standing on Sundays and throughout the Paschal season.

Inasmuch as there are certain persons who kneel in prayer upon the Lord's Day and in the season from Easter to Pentecost, the holy Synod, desirous to obtain uniformity in the observance of all forms of worship in every diocese, has seen fit to decree that they offer their prayers to God standing.

II. CREED AND CANONS OF THE SECOND GENERAL COUNCIL, HELD AT CONSTANTINOPLE, A. D., 381.

1. THE CREED AS REVISED BY THE COUNCIL OF CONSTANTINOPLE, ACCORDING TO THE TEXT CONTAINED IN THE ACTS OF THE COUNCIL OF CHALCEDON.

We believe in one God, the FATHER Almighty, Maker of heaven and earth and of all things visible and invisible. And in one Lord JESUS CHRIST, the only-begotten Son of God, begotten of the Father before all worlds [*aeons,*] Light of Light, very God of very God, begotten, not made, being of one substance with the Father; by whom all things were made; who for us men, and for our salvation, came down from heaven, and was incarnate by the Holy Ghost of the Virgin Mary, and was made man; he was crucified for us under Pontius Pilate, and suffered, and was buried, and the third day he rose again, according to the Scriptures, and ascended into heaven, and sitteth on the right hand of the Father; from thence he shall come again, with glory, to judge the quick and the dead; whose kingdom shall have no end. And in the HOLY GHOST, the Lord and Giver of life, who precedeth from the Father, who with the Father and the Son together is worshipped and glorified, who spake by the prophets. In one holy catholic and apostolic church; we acknowledge one baptism for the remission of sins; we look for the resurrection of the dead, and the life of the world to come. Amen.

2. SUBJECTS OF THE CANONS.

1. The Nicene faith must be maintained, and all heresies anathematized.
2. All bishops to observe their existing limits of jurisdiction.
3. The bishop of Constantinople to have priority next after the bishop of Rome.
4. Against Maximus, the pretender to the see of Constantinople.
5. [A. D. 382?] On reception of Antiochenes professing the true faith.
6. [A. D. 382?] On accusations against bishops.
[7. Spurious. On the mode of receiving converts from heresy.]

3. CANONS OF THE FIRST COUNCIL OF CONSTANTINOPLE.

CANON 1. *The Nicene faith must be maintained, and all heresies anathematized.*

The confession of faith of the three hundred and eighteen fathers assembled at Nicæa in Bithynia shall not be set aside, but shall remain authoritative, and every heresy shall be anathematized, especially the Eunomian or Anomaean, the Arian or Eudoxian, the Semi-Arian or Pneumatomachian, the Sabellian, the Marcellian, the Photinian and the Apollinarian.

CANON 2. *All bishops to observe their existing limits of jurisdiction.*

The bishops of one diocese shall not visit the churches of another and make confusion among them; but, in accordance with the canons, the bishop of Alexandria shall govern Egypt only, those of the East, the East only, while at the same time regarding the privileges of the church at Antioch, as granted in the canons of Nicæa. And the bishops of Asia shall have jurisdiction over Asia only, those of Pontus, over Pontus only, and those of Thrace, over Thrace only. Unless summoned, bishops shall not go outside their dioceses for the purpose of ordination, or other ecclesiastical functions. But, while the existing canon regarding the dioceses is observed, it is clear that in each province the provincial Synod is to rule, according to the decisions of Nicæa. And the churches of God among the barbaric nations shall be governed according to the custom which prevailed in the times of the fathers.

CANON 3. The bishop of Constantinople to have priority next after the bishop of Rome.

Next to the bishop of Rome, the bishop of Constantinople shall have highest rank, because Constantinople is New Rome.

CANON 4. Against Maximus, the pretender to the see of Constantinople.

As to Maximus the Cynic and the disorder in Constantinople occasioned by him, [be it known that] Maximus never really became bishop, and is not one now, neither are those who have been ordained by him, whatever their rank in the clergy, really ordained, since all things performed upon him [i. e. his ordination as bishop] and by him are pronounced invalid.

CANON 5. [A. D. 382?] On reception of Antiochenes professing the true faith.

Concerning the "tome of the western [Christians"], we also have recognized all Antiochians as orthodox who acknowledge the oneness of the Godhead of the Father, the Son, and the Holy Ghost.

CANON 6. [A. D. 382?] On accusations against bishops.

Inasmuch as many, to disturb and subvert the order of the church, maliciously and falsely invent charges against the orthodox bishops of the church, for no reason but to injure the reputation of the priests and introduce trouble among the peaceable people, the holy Synod assembled at Constantinople decrees that in future no accuser shall be admitted without examination; that neither all shall be permitted nor all forbidden to make charges against the rulers of the church. But, in case of a private charge against the bishop, as of fraud or any other injustice, no examination shall be made as to the person or the religion of the accuser; for the conscience of the bishop should be clear, and he who alleges injustice, whatever his religion, should receive his just dues. But if the complaint against the bishop is of an ecclesiastical nature, then the persons of the accusers must be considered, in order first, that heretics may not be allowed to bring charges concerning ecclesiastical matters against the orthodox bishops. By heretics are meant both those formerly shut out from the church, and those afterward anathematized by us. In addition to these, also those who indeed profess to hold the sound faith, but who have separated themselves and hold meetings in opposition to our canonical bishops. Again, members of the church who have been for any cause condemned and excommunicated, or have been deprived of communion, whether clergy or laity, shall not be allowed to accuse a bishop until they have first cleared themselves of the charge against them. In like manner, those under accusation may not accuse a bishop, or any of the clergy, until they have shown themselves innocent of the charges against them. If, however, persons other than heretics, excommunicated, condemned or accused, bring a charge on ecclesiastical matters against the bishop, the holy Synod orders that such shall first bring their complaints before the assembled bishops of the province, and before them prove their charges. Then if the bishops of the province are not in position to punish the bishop for the offences charged, the accusers shall carry it over to a greater synod of the bishops of the diocese, called for the purpose, and they shall not make the complaint before they have in writing promised to undergo the same punishment [as would the bishop if guilty], in case they are proved on examination to have falsely accused him. If, ignoring these clear directions, anyone should presume to assail the ear of the emperor, or the secular courts, or an ecumenical council and so show disrespect to the bishops of his diocese, his charge shall most certainly not be received; because he has shown contempt for the canons and violated the order of the church.

CANON 7. [Spurious. On the mode of receiving converts from heresy.]

Those who come over to orthodoxy and from heretics to the number of the saved, we receive in the following prescribed manner. Arians, Macedonians, Sabbatians, Novatians [who call themselves Katharoi and Aristeroi], Quartodecimans or Tetradites, and Apollinarians, we receive after they have presented written petitions and have anathematized every heresy not agreeing with the holy catholic and apostolic church of God. First, they are sealed or anointed with the holy oil on the forehead, the eyes, nostrils, mouth and ears; and as we seal them we say, "The seal of the gift of the Holy Spirit." But Eunomians, who only baptize with one immersion, Montanists, here called Phrygians, Sabellians, who teach the identity of the Father and the Son and make some other grievous errors, and all other heretics [since there are many here, especially from Galatia]—all wishing to come from these to orthodoxy, we receive as we do pagans. The first day we make them

Christians, the second catechumens, the third day we exorcise them after three times breathing on the forehead and on the ears. And so we give them instruction and make them attend church for a long period and listen to the Scriptures, and then we baptize them.

III. THE CANONS OF THE THIRD GENERAL COUNCIL, HELD AT EPHESUS, A. D. 431.

1. SUBJECTS OF THE CANONS.

1. Against metropolitans joining the rival council, or the Pelagian party.
2. Against bishops adhering to, or going over to the rival council.
3. In favor of orthodox clerics deposed by Nestorian party, or belonging to dioceses of Nestorianizing bishops.
4. Against clerics adopting Nestorianism or Pelegianism.
5. Against clerics deposed for misconduct and uncanonically restored by Nestorius.
6. Against all who resist decrees of the council.
7. No new creed to be composed or presented to converts.
8. Church of Cyprus, and all churches to retain existing rights.

2. CANONS OF THE COUNCIL OF EPHESUS.

CANON 1. Against metropolitans joining the rival council, or the Pelagian party.

Inasmuch as those who were for any cause absent from the holy synod should not be ignorant of the affairs there transacted concerning them, be it known to your holiness and love that if a metropolitan of the province has turned from this holy ecumenical Synod and joined the ranks of the apostate, or shall afterward join them; or has accepted the beliefs of Coelestius [i. e. the Pelagians] or shall accept them, he has no longer any jurisdiction over the bishops of the province, and is already excluded from all church fellowship by the Synod, and without power; but it is also the duty of the bishops of the province and the neighboring orthodox metropolitans to remove him entirely from the rank of the episcopate.

CANON 2. *Against bishops adhering to, or going over to the rival council.*

If any of the provincial bishops did not attend the holy Synod, but went over to the apostates, or attempted to go over; or if they subscribed to the deposition of Nestorius and then afterward went over to the ranks of the apostate; these shall be entirely deposed from the priesthood and stripped of their office.

CANON 3. *In favor of orthodox clerics deposed by Nestorian party, or belonging to dioceses of Nestorianizing bishops.*

If any of the clergy, in city or country, have, owing to their orthodox faith, been rejected from the priesthood by Nestorius and his party, they shall resume their office; and, in general, the clergy who agree with the orthodox and ecumenical Synod are enjoined not to submit in any respect to apostate or apostatizing bishops.

CANON 4. *Against clerics adopting Nestorianism or Pelagianism.*

If any of the clergy shall apostatize and presume publicly or privately to adhere to Nestorius or Coelestius, they shall be deposed from their rank by the holy Synod.

CANON 5. *Against clerics deposed for misconduct and uncanonically restored by Nestorius.*

Those who for improper actions have been condemned by the holy Synod or by their own bishops, and whom Nestorius and his party in their usual lax fashion have afterwards attempted to restore to fellowship or rank, or shall attempt to restore, shall remain unbenefited thereby and unrestored to rank.

CANON 6. *Against all who resist decrees of the Council.*

Now in general, if any presume in any way to resist any of the enactments of the holy Synod at Ephesus, the holy Synod decrees that they shall be utterly deprived of their office, if they be bishops or other clerics; and if laymen, they shall be excommunicated.

The decree of the holy Synod pronounced after reading first the creed of the three hundred and eighteen holy and blessed fathers at Nicæa and then the impious and false creed written by Theodore of Mopsuestia, which latter was exposed in the holy Synod at Ephesus by ˙sios presbyter of Philadelphia.

CANON 7. No new creed to be composed or presented to converts.

These things having been read the holy Synod decreed that it was not permitted to any one to recite, or to compose, or to proffer any other creed than that appointed by the holy fathers under the guidance of the Holy Spirit in the city of Nicæa.

Moreover, those who shall dare to compose, or to bring forward, or to proffer another creed to such as are willing to turn to a knowledge of the truth, whether from among the Greeks, or the Jews, or any heresy whatsoever, these shall be deposed, if they are bishops or clerics; the bishops from their bishoprics, the clerics from the clericate; if laymen, they shall be anathematized. In like manner, if any individuals, whether bishops, clerics or laymen, shall be detected thinking or teaching those things contained in the creed exposed by Charisios, the presbyter, concerning the only begotten Son of God, or those wicked and perverted doctrines of Nestorius, they shall be subject to the decree of this holy and ecumenical Synod. It is accordingly clear that the bishop is to be dismissed from the episcopate, and degraded. And the cleric likewise is to be cut off from the clericate. But if the person be a layman, let him be anathematized in accordance with what has been said.

Vote of this holy Synod given upon the appeal made to it by the bishops of Cyprus.

CANON 8. Church of Cyprus, and all churches to retain existing rights.

A matter not covered by the ecclesiastical laws and the canons of the holy apostles, and affecting the liberty of all, has been brought before us by our fellow bishop, Rheginus, beloved of God, together with Zeno and Evagrius, beloved of God, bishops of the province of Cyprus. Wherefore, as ordinary ailments need strong medicines, and serious troubles result in real harm, and the worst diseases are fatal, if their course is not at once stayed, so the bishop of the city of Antioch, having performed ordinations in Cyprus, the devout men composing the holy Synod accordingly declare in response to petitions and personal requests, that the representatives of the holy churches of Cyprus have the indisputable and inviolable right, in accordance with the canons of the holy fathers and ancient custom, to themselves ordain their own most pious bishops. Moreover, the same rights shall be preserved to other dioceses and to all other provinces everywhere, so that no one bishops, beloved of God, may invade another province, which previously and even from the beginning been under his care or that of his predecessors. But if any one shall occupy or take a diocese by his own power, it shall be surrendered; in order that the statutes of the fathers may not be broken, lest the arrogance of worldly power creep into the sacred functions, lest we in our ignorance utterly destroy the liberty, which our Lord Jesus Christ, the Redeemer of all men, purchased for us by his own blood. It is therefore agreeable to this holy and ecumenical Synod that the rights of each province, possessed from the beginning, shall be preserved pure and inviolate, so that each metropolitan, having obtained his functions in a proper manner may exercise his office in security. Now if any one shall bring forward a decision contrary to these ordinances, it is clear to this holy and ecumenical Synod that the same is without force.

IV. DEFINITION OF FAITH AND CANONS OF THE FOURTH CENERAL COUNCIL OF CHALCEDON, A. D. 451.

1. DEFINITION OF THE FAITH BY THE COUNCIL OF CHALCEDON.

The holy and great and ecumenical Synod, which by the grace of God and the decree of our most pious and Christian Emperors, Marcian and Valentinian, is convened in the metropolis Chalcedon of the province of Bythinia, in the chapel of the holy and pure martyr Euphemia, has defined as follows:

Our Lord and Savior Jesus Christ, when confirming the faith in his disciples, declared: 'Peace I leave with you: my peace I give unto you,' so that no one might be in disagreement with his neighbor concerning the doctrines of religion, but that the preaching of the truth might be made known to all alike. Inasmuch, however, as the evil one ceases not by his tares to choke out the seeds of religion, and is ever devising something new in opposition to the truth, God has therefore, in his care for the human race, stirred up zeal in this pious and orthodox Emperor to call together unto himself the heads of the priesthood, so that the grace of Christ, the Lord of us all, being operative, every plague of falsehood may be removed from the sheep of Christ and they --- be nourished with tender plants of truth. This we have accordingly done, since we have expelled by our common judgment the doctrines of error, have renewed the right faith of the fathers, have proclaimed the creed of the 318 to all, and have subscribed to that statement of religion adopted by those fathers who afterward gathered in the great city of Constantinople, a hundred and fifty strong; this faith we ourselves ratify. While guarding the order and form of faith everywhere current and ourselves receiving the regulations of the earlier holy Ephesian Synod, of which Coelestine of Rome and Cyril of Alexandria, sainted to memory, were the guides, we declare that the confession of the 318 holy and blessed fathers who gathered under the Emperor Constantine, of sainted memory, is a light to the right and unblemished faith; and affirm that that is also valid which was decreed by the 150 holy fathers in Constantinople in repudiation of those engendering heresy, and for the confirmation of our own catholic and apostolic faith. [Here follow the Creeds of Nicæa and Constantinople.] This wise and wholesome symbol of divine grace should indeed suffice for a complete knowledge and confirmation of religion, since it teaches the finalities concerning the Father and the Son and the Holy Spirit, and offers the incarnation of the Lord to those who receive it in faith. As, however, those who attempt to do away with the preaching of the truth have devised vain expressions through their own heresies, daring indeed to destroy the mystery of the dispensation [incarnation] of our Lord, and rejecting the designation "God-bearer" as applied to the Virgin; moreover, introducing an inter-mixture and fusion [of natures], imagining without reason that there is only one nature of the flesh and the Godhead, and rashly maintaining that the divine nature of the Only-begotten through the mixture became passible. Wherefore, desiring to exclude every machination against the truth, the present holy, great and ecumenical Synod, teaching afresh the stability of the proclamation, decrees in the first place that the faith of the 318 holy fathers shall remain inviolate, and also that the doctrine concerning the essence of the Holy Spirit, afterwards promulgated by the 150 holy fathers gathered in the royal city in opposition to the Pneumatomachi, shall have equal validity. This they made known to all, not as though supplying any deficiency in preceeding deliverances, but in order to make known in writing their deep conviction concerning the Holy Spirit in opposition to such as seek to set aside his glory. On account of those, however, who attempted destroy the mystery of the dispensation [incarnation], and shamel spoke of him who was born of the holy Mary as a mere man, the S has accepted as valid the synodal letters of the blessed Cyril, pastor of the church of Alexandria, to Nestorius and to the orientals in refutation of the blasphemies of Nestorius, and as expressive of the deep conviction of those seeking with holy zeal to preserve the redemptive symbol; and it has added to them the letter of the president of the great and ancient church of Rome, the blessed and holy archbishop Leo, written to the sainted archbishop Flavian for the overthrow of the errors of Eutyches, as agreeing with the doctrine of the great Peter, and as a firm pillar against all heretics, for the proper confirmation of the orthodox dogmas. The Synod opposes those who attempt to sever the sacred mystery of the dispensation [incarnation] into a duality of sons; and it excludes from the sacred fellowship those who dare to speak of the Godhead of the Only-begotten as passible, and withstands those who imagine, in regard to Christ's two natures, a commixture or fusion, and expels those who foolishly affirm that the 'form of a servant' which Christ assumed from us was of a heavenly or any other [non-human] essence; and it anathematizes those who fable that there were two natures of the Lord before the union, but make out that there was only one after the union. Following therefore the holy fathers, we all unanimously instruct men to confess one and the same Son, our Lord Jesus Christ, the same perfect in Godhead, the same perfect in manhood; truly God and truly man; the same of a reasonable soul and a body, coessential with the Father according to the Godhead, the same also coessential with us according to the manhood, 'in all points like unto us, apart from sin;' before the ages begotten of the Father according to the Godhead, and in the last days, for us and for our salvation, the same [was born] of Mary the Virgin, the Mother of God, according to the manhood; one and the same Christ, Son, Lord, Only-begotten: acknowledged as in two natures, without amalgamation, without change, without division, without severance. The difference of the nature has not only not been destroyed by reason of the union, but rather the peculiarity of each nature has been preserved, combining indeed into one person and one hypostasis; not as though divided or separated into two persons, but as one and the same Son and Only-begotten God-Logos, the Lord Jesus Christ. Just as the prophets announced him and he himself, the Lord Jesus Christ, taught us, and the creed of the fathers has handed down to us. These things therefore having been defined by us with all possible exactness and care, the holy ecumenical Synod has decreed, that none shall advance, or write, or compose, or think, or teach others another creed; and those daring to compose, or bring forward, or teach, or give another symbol to such as desire to turn from Hellenism, or Judaism, or any heresy whatsoever to a knowledge of the truth, they, if they be bishops or clerics, shall be deposed, the bishops from their bishoprics, the clerics from the clericate; but if they be monks or laymen, they shall be excommunicated. Upon the reading of the decree all the bishops were delighted and exclaimed: 'This is the faith of the fathers! The metropolitans must now subscribe while the imperial commissioners are here; definitions so good can allow of no delay; this is the faith of the apostles, we all agree to it, we all think thus!' The august and glorious commissioners said: 'These things having been defined by the holy fathers, and being agreeable to all, shall now go to his divine majesty, the Emperor.

2. SUBJECTS OF THE CANONS.

1. Preceding canons ratified.
2. Against simoniacal ordinations.
3. Clerics not to undertake secular business.
4. Against disorderly conduct in monks.
5. Bishops and clerics not to migrate.
6. None to be ordained without a title.
7. Clerics and monks to hold no secular office.
8. Clergy of monasteries, etc., to be subject to their bishops.
9. On the prosecution of causes by clerics or bishops.
10. Against pluralities.
11. Letters of peace to be furnished to needy travellers.
12. No new 'metropolis' to be erected by civil authority.
13. Foreign clerics to produce letters commendatory.
14. On the marriage of readers and singers.
15. On deaconesses.
16. No monk or dedicated virgin to marry.
17. On questions as to diocesan limits.
18. Against conspiracies of clerics or monks.
19. Provincial synods to meet regularly.
20. On accusations of bishops or clerics.
22. A bishop's property not to be taken away at his death.
23. Clerics and monks not to make a disorderly stay in

24. Monasteries not be secularised.
25. Consecrations of bishops not to be delayed.
26. All bishops to have stewards of church property.
27. Against seizure of women under pretext of marriage.
28. On the dignity and powers of the see of Constantinople.
[29. Bishops not to be degraded to the order of presbyters.]
[30. On the case of the Egyptian bishops.]

3. CANONS OF THE COUNCIL OF CHALCEDON.

CANON 1. Preceding canons ratified.

We have judged it proper that the canons, promulgated by the holy fathers in each Synod until the present, remain in force.

CANON 2. Against simoniacal ordinations.

If any bishop shall hold an ordination for money, and shall put on sale that grace which is not to be sold; if then, he ordain for money a bishop, or chorepiscopos [rural bishop], or presbyter, or deacon, or any man who is numbered among the clergy, or if he shall appoint for money a steward, or advocate [defensor], or sacristan [?], or in short any one enrolled upon the canon, on account of his own love of sordid gain:—the bishop who is convicted of attempting such a thing will imperil his own clerical position; and the person ordained shall derive no advantage from the ordination or appointment thus venially obtained, but must be removed from the dignity, or office which he has acquired for money. And further, if any man is plainly seen to be a third party to bargains so shameful and nefarious, he also must be deposed from his own rank, if he is a cleric, and if a layman, or monk, he must be anathematized.

CANON 3. Clerics not to undertake secular business.

It has come to the holy Synod that certain men who are registered among the clergy become, through their own love of base gain, farmers of other men's estates, and contract for managing worldly affairs, thus becoming remiss in the service of God; that they also insinuate themselves into the houses of worldly persons, and in covetousness accept the management of their property: therefore the holy and great Synod has decreed that in future no bishop, or cleric, or monk shall either farm estates, or administer property, or intrude himself into secular administrations, except when he is legally compelled to assume the guardianship of minors, or is entrusted by the bishop with the care of ecclesiastical business, or of orphans, or of widows not otherwise provided for, and in general of persons who most need help from the church, on account of the fear of the Lord. Now if any one in future attempts to transgress these decrees, he shall incur the ecclesiastical penalties.

CANON 4. Against disorderly conduct in monks.

Those who truly and unfeignedly follow the monastic life should be deemed worthy of fitting honor. But inasmuch as certain men assume the monastic state as a pretext and disturb the churches and the affairs of state, wandering about the cities heedlessly, and, not content with that, even undertaking to found monasteries of their own, it is hereby decreed that no one shall anywhere build or found a monastery, or oratory, against the will of the bishop of the city; also, that the monks in each city and rural district be in subjection to the bishops, and cling to a quiet life and attend to fasting and prayer only, continuing in the places where they renounced [the world]. Nor may they annoyingly intrude into the affairs of the church, or of this life, or have anything to do with them, leaving their own monasteries [in order to do so], unless they be permitted by the bishop of the city for some necessary reason; and they may not receive into their monasteries a slave who wishes to lead a monastic life contrary to the will of his own master. And they who transgress this ordinance, we have decreed to be excommunicated, that the name of God be not blasphemed. The bishop of the city, then, ought to make requisite provision for the monasteries.

CANON 5. Bishops and clerics not to migrate.

With regard to bishops or clerics who remove from city to city, it has seemed best that the canons enacted by the holy fathers, which apply to their case, shall retain their original force.

CANON 6. None to be ordained without a title.

No one shall be ordained at large, either to the presbyterate, or diaconate, or to any place in the ecclesiastical order whatsoever: on the contrary the person ordained must be particularly designated to some church in city, or village, or to some oratory [martyr's chapel], or monastery. Such ordination at large, then, the holy Synod has decreed to be null and nowhere operative, to the disgrace of the ordainer.

CANON 7. Clerics and monks to hold no secular office.

We have decreed that those who have been once registered among the clergy, or who have become monks, must enter upon neither public service nor any other secular calling; or if they have the temerity to do so, and do not penitently return to that life which they formerly chose for God's sake, they are to be anathematized.

CANON 8. Clergy of monasteries, etc., to be subject to their bishops.

In accordance with the tradition of the holy fathers, the clerics in almshouses, monasteries, and martyries must remain under the jurisdiction of the bishop of the city where they live, and must not in self-will grow restive under the authority of their own bishop. And those who dare to violate this statute in any way whatsoever, and do not subject themselves to their own bishop, must, if they are clerics, incur canonical penalties, or if monks or laymen, be excommunicated.

CANON 9. On the prosecution of causes by clerics or bishops.

If a cleric has a matter against another cleric, he must not leave his own bishop and run away to secular tribunals; but he must first lay the charge before his own bishop, or, with the bishop's own consent, before those whom both parties are willing to make arbiters of the matter in dispute. Now if any man does otherwise in such a case, he shall incur canonical penalties. And if any cleric has a matter against his own, or another bishop, the case must be tried in the provincial synod; but if a bishop or cleric has a dispute with the metropolitan of the same province, he must go to the exarch of the dioecesis [the superior metropolitan], or to the see of the imperial city, Constantinople, and have the case there adjudicated.

Canon 10. Against pluralities.

A cleric is not permitted to be registered in two cities at once, viz: in the church in which he was originally ordained, and in that to which, through love of empty glory, he has fled, presumably because it is larger; and those who have done this thing, must be restored to their own church in which they were ordained at the first, and must there minister. If, however, a man has really been transferred from one church to another, he must have nothing more to do with the affairs of the former church, or with the martyries, or almshouses, or hospices under its jurisdiction. The holy Synod has therefore decreed, that those who are so bold as to do anything thus forbidden, after the publication of the ordinance of this great and ecumenical Synod, must be deposed from their rank.

Canon 11. Letters of peace to be furnished to needy travellers.

We have decreed that all poor persons, and such as need assistance, shall after an examination travel with ecclesiastical letters of peace simply, and not with letters of commendation; because it is seemly that commendatory letters should be granted only to persons held in high esteem.

Canon 12. No new 'metropolis' to be erected by civil authority.

It has come to our notice that some, in defiance of ecclesiastical enactments, have made applications to the government and, with the authority of pragmatic letters, have divided one province into two, in this way constituting two metropolitans in the same province. The holy Synod has therefore decreed, that in future no bishop be so bold as to do this, for any one who attempts it must be degraded from the position which he holds; and all the cities, which, by imperial edicts have been honored with the name of "metropolis," may enjoy the honorary title only, as also their ruling bishops. The peculiar right of the real metropolis must of course be conserved.

Canon 13. Foreign clerics to produce letters commendatory.

Foreign clerics and leaders must not, by any means, be allowed to officiate anywhere in another city without the authorization of commendatory letters from their own bishop.

CANON 14. *On the marriage of readers and singers.*

Inasmuch as in certain provinces readers and singers are permitted to marry, the holy Synod has decreed that at least no one shall be allowed to take a heterodox wife. And those who have already begotten children of such a marriage, must bring their offspring into the communion of the catholic church, if they had previously caused them to be baptized among the heretics; if, however, their children have not been thus baptized, they may not henceforth have them baptized among the heretics, nor unite them in marriage to a heretic, or a Jew, or a pagan, unless indeed the person joined to the orthodox spouse promises to turn to the orthodox faith. Now if any one transgresses this ordinance of the holy Synod, he shall incur canonical discipline.

CANON. 15. *On deaconesses.*

A woman may not be ordained a deaconess before forty years of age, and then only after thorough scrutiny. If, then, after receiving ordination, and remaining at her duty for some time, she entangle herself in marriage, thus doing despite unto the grace of God, she must be anathematized, and her husband along with her.

CANON 16. *No monk or dedicated virgin to marry.*

A virgin who has consecrated herself to the Lord God, and likewise also monks, are not permitted to enter into the marriage relation: and if any be found so doing, they must be excommunicated. Yet we have decreed that the bishop of the place has authority to use clemency in their case.

CANON 17. *On questions as to diocesan limits.*

The rural or country parishes in each church should remain undisturbed under the authority of the bishop who holds them, especially if he has ruled them in peaceable possession for the space of thirty years. But if, within the thirty years, a dispute about them has arisen, he who says he is wronged is permitted to bring the matter before the provincial synod. But if a man is wronged by his own metropolitan, the case must be tried before the exarch of the diocese, or the see of Constantinople, as we have before directed. And if any city has been rebuilt by imperial authority, or shall be in the future, the arrangement of the church dioceses must follow the political and public models.

CANON 18. *Against conspiracies of clerics or monks.*

The crime of conspiracy, or faction has been totally prohibited, even by the civil laws: much more seemly is it, then, that the church of God should forbid it. If then, any clerics or monks shall be found conspiring, or forming factions, or concocting plots against bishops, or fellow clerics, they must lose their office.

CANON 19. *Provincial synods to meet regularly.*

It has come to our ears that in the provinces the synods of bishops provided for by the statute are not held, and, as a result, many ecclesiastical matters which need correcting escape attention: the holy Synod has therefore decreed, that in accordance with the canons of the holy fathers the bishops in each province shall assemble twice a year, wherever the bishop of the metropolis thinks best, and that they shall correct each abuse that arises: also, that those bishops who do not attend, though they are residing in their own cities at the time and are in good health and are not engaged in any unavoidable and necessary occupation, shall receive a brotherly rebuke.

As we have before decreed, clerics belonging to any church must not be allowed to connect themselves with a church in another city, but must be content with the one in which they were originally deemed worthy to minister, though this rule does not apply to those who, having lost their own country, have been compelled to migrate to another church. If then any bishop, after hearing this ordinance, shall receive a cleric belonging to another bishop, we have decided that both receiver and received shall be excommunicated until such time as the deserting cleric shall return to his own church.

CANON 20. *On accusations of bishops or clerics.*

Clerics or laymen who bring charges against bishops or clerics must not be allowed to make a formal accusation indiscriminately and without examination, but must first have their own characters tested.

CANON 22. *A bishop's property not to be taken away at his death.*

Clerics must not be allowed, after the death of their bishop, to plunder his effects, an act forbidden by the ancient canons also. Those, then, who do this, risk their positions.

CANON 23. *Clerics and monks not to make a disorderly stay in Constantinople.*

It has come to the ears of the holy Synod that certain clerics and monks, though entrusted with no business by their bishop, and sometimes after having been excommunicated by him, betake themselves to the imperial city [Constantinople] and remain long there, making disturbances and troubling the order of the church, and even upsetting some households. The holy Synod has therefore decreed that notice be given to such persons by the advocate of the most holy church of Constantinople to depart from the imperial city, and if they impudently continue such conduct, that they be ejected by the advocate, even against their will, and betake themselves to the places where they belong.

CANON 24. *Monasteries not be secularised.*

Monasteries once consecrated with the consent of the bishop must remain monasteries forever, and their property must be preserved for them; nor may they ever be converted into secular dwellings; those, then, who give their consent to such secularization will incur the penalties prescribed by the canons.

CANON 25. *Consecrations of bishops not to be delayed.*

Inasmuch as some of the metropolitans, as we have heard reported on all sides, are neglectful of the flocks entrusted to them, and defer the ordination of bishops, the holy Synod has been pleased to decree that the ordination of bishops take place within three months after a vacancy, unless some unavoidable necessity prevails to lengthen the interval. Now if a metropolitan does not do as here directed, he will incur ecclesiastical punishment. The income, however, of the church thus widowed by the death of the bishop, must be safely kept by the steward of the church.

CANON 26. All bishops to have stewards of church property.

Inasmuch as in certain churches, as we have heard widely reported, the bishops administer the church property without the aid of stewards, it has been resolved that every church which has a bishop, should also have a steward of its own clerical stall, who shall manage the church's funds in accordance with the judgment of his bishop, in order that the financial management of the church may not be unattested, and, as a result, the church property squandered, and reproach be cast upon the priesthood. If, then, the bishop will not do this, he must be punished according to the sacred canons.

CANON 27. Against seizure of women under pretext of marriage.

Those who ravish women even under the pretence of marriage, or who are accomplices in the whole plan of the ravishers, or in the act itself, the holy Synod has decreed shall fall from their office, if clerics, and be anathematized, if laymen.

CANON 28. On the dignity and powers of the see of Constantinople.

Following in all respects the decrees of the holy fathers, and recognizing the canon just read, which was framed by the 150 most religious bishops, who assembled in the queen city, Constantinople, New Rome, in the reign of the emperor Theodosius, of pious memory, we also so decree and vote as they did respecting the privileges of the most holy church of this same Constantinople, New Rome. For the fathers accorded the privileges to the see of the Elder Rome with good reason, since she was then the imperial city; and the 150 most religious bishops, acting upon the same principle, awarded the same privileges to the most holy see of the new Rome, rightly judging that a city which is honored with the sovereignty and senate, and which enjoys equal privileges with the elder queen city, Rome, should receive dignity like hers in matters ecclesiastical as well, holding the place next to her: And so that the metropolitans only of the dioceses of Pontus, Asia and Thrace, together with those bishops in their dioceses who are settled over barbarians, shall be ordained by the aforesaid most holy see of the most holy church at Constantinople, each metropolitan of the aforesaid dio-

the bishops of that province, as the sacred canons prescribe. But, as we have said before, the metropolitans of the aforesaid dioceses are to be ordained by the archbishop of Constantinople, after harmonious elections have been held, in accordance with the usage, and the result reported to him.

CANON [29. Bishops not to be degraded to the order of presbyters.]

To change a bishop to the rank of a presbyter is sacrilege. If any just cause removes bishops from episcopal functions, they ought not to hold the position even of presbyter. But if they are removed from their high office without having some charge proved against them, they shall be restored to their episcopal rank.

CANON [30. On the case of the Egyptian bishops.]

Inasmuch as the most pious bishops of Egypt have up to the present time postponed subscribing to the letters of the most holy archbishop Leo, not in a spirit of opposition to the catholic faith, but upon the plea that they have a custom in the Egyptian diocese to do nothing of this kind contrary to the will and direction of the archbishop, and since they ask that indulgence be granted to them until the ordination of the future bishop of the great city of the Alexandrians; it has seemed to us reasonable and humane, that such indulgence be granted to them, while they remain [still in full possession of their episcopal status] within the imperial city, until the archbishop of the great city of the Alexandrians shall be ordained.

V. SOURCES AND LITERATURE.

TEXTS OF THE CANONS.

Harduini, Collectio Conciliorum (Par. 1715 seq.)

Mansi, Collectio sacrorum Conciliorum (Flor. 1759 seq.)

Routh, Scriptorum Eccl. Opuscula. (1832).

Hefele, Conciliengeschichte, (1855 ff. English Trans. 1872 f.)

Bright, Canons of the First Four Councils, with notes. (Oxford, 2nd Ed. 1892.)

LITERATURE:

Histories (General, or of the Church, of the Councils, of Christian Doctrine, of the Creeds, of the Person of Christ, of Heresies, etc.) by Baronius, Petavius, Tillemont, Bingham, Walch, Assemani, Fleury, Schroeckh, Gibbon, Neander, Gieseler, Baur, Broglie, Hagenbach, Rothe, Hefele, Kaye, Landon, Milman, Newman, Dorner, Shedd, Schaff, Stanley, Neale, Hort, Swainson, Moeller, Sohm, Harnack, Bury, Brightman. The standard Encyclopedias, Dictionaries, etc., should be consulted.

SERIES FOR 1894.

I. Early Reformation Period in England.* Single number, 20 pages.
II. Urban and the Crusaders.† Single number, 24 pages.
III. The Reaction after 1815.* Single number, 24 pages.
IV. Letters of the Crusaders.* Double number, 40 pages.
V. The French Revolution, 1789-1791.* Double number, 36 pages.
VI. English Constitutional Documents.* Double number, 36 pages.

SERIES FOR 1895.

I. English Towns and Gilds. Double number, 40 pages.
II. Napoleon and Europe. Double number, 32 pages.
III. The Mediæval Student. Single number, 20 pages.
IV. Monastic Tales of the XIII Century. Single number, 20 pages.
V. England in the Time of Wycliffe. Single number, 20 pages.
VI. Period of Early Reformation in Germany. Double number, 32 pages.
VII. Life of St. Columban. Double number, 36 pages.

SERIES FOR 1896.

I. The Fourth Crusade. Single number, 20 pages.
II. Statistical Documents of the Middle Ages. Single number, 23 pages.
III. Period of the Later Reformation. Double number, 32 pages.
IV. The Witch-Persecutions. Double number, 36 pages.
V. English Manorial Documents. Double number, 32 pages.
VI. The Pre-Reformation Period. Double number, 34 pages.

SERIES FOR 1897.

I. The Early Christian Persecutions. Double number, 32 pages.
II. Canons and Creeds of the First Four Councils. Double number, 31 pages.
III. Documents Illustrative of Feudalism. Double number, 36 pages.
IV. Ordeals, Compurgation, Excommunication, and Interdict. Double number, 34 pages.
V. Typical Cahiers of 1789. Double number, 36 pages.

SERIES FOR 1898.

I. Monumentum Ancyranum. (About 96 pages.) Ready in May.
II. Remonstrance of the *Cour des Aides*, May, 1775. (About 100 pages.) Ready in November.

Annual subscription, $1.00.
Single numbers, Vol. I, 15 cents; Vols. II, III and IV, 10 cents.
Double numbers, Vol. I, 25 cents; Vols. II, III and IV, 20 cents.
Numbers in Vol. V, unbound, 60 cents each; bound, 80 cents, each.
Bound Volumes, $1.50.
Discounts will be given on orders for 25 or more numbers.
Subscriptions and orders should be sent to

DANA C. MUNRO,

UNIVERSITY OF PENNSYLVANIA,

May, 1898. Philadelphia, Pa.

Translations and Reprints

FROM THE

Original Sources of European History

DOCUMENTS ILLUSTRATIVE OF FEUDALISM.

EDITED BY EDWARD P. CHEYNEY, A.M.

PUBLISHED BY

The Department of History of the University of Pennsylvania.

Philadelphia, Pa., 1898.

ENGLISH AGENCY: P. S. KING & SON, 12-14 King Street, London, S. W.

Price, 20 Cents.

THE use by readers and students of those original documents from which our knowledge of history is so largely drawn has come to be valued in recent times at something like its true worth. The sequence of past events, the form and spirit of institutions, the characters of men, the prevailing habits of thought, obtain their greatest reality when we study them in the very words used by the men to whom the past was the living present. Even historians who have not been characterized by a close dependence on the results of patient investigation of the sources have recognized the superiority of an appeal to original testimony. Mr. Froude says, "Whenever possible, let us not be told about this man or that. Let us hear the man himself speak, let us see him act, and let us be left to form our own opinion about him." And in "Stones of Venice," Mr. Ruskin writes, "the only history worth reading is that written at the time of which it treats, the history of what was done and seen, heard out of the mouths of the men who did and saw. One fresh draught of such history is worth more than a thousand volumes of abstracts, and reasonings, and suppositions and theories."

Experience has proved, not only that the interest of students can be more readily obtained through the vividness of a direct and first-hand presentation, and that knowledge thus gained is more tangible and exact; but that the critical judgment is developed in no slight degree, and the ability as well as the interest for further study thus secured.

The utilization of the original sources of history has, however, been much restricted by their comparative inaccessibility. A great proportion of such documents as illustrate European history exist only in more or less unfamiliar languages; many are to be found only in large and expensive collections, or in works that are out of print and therefore difficult to obtain or consult.

The desire to overcome in some degree this inaccessibility, especially for their own classes, led the editors of the present series of translations and reprints from the original sources of European history to undertake its publication. During the past three years evidence has been given of the usefulness of the documents in several directions. Their most considerable use has naturally been with college classes. One or more of the issues has been used in twenty-five of the principal Universities and Colleges, and four Divinity Schools. In addition to these and their use in lower schools they have been found to give increased value to University Extension courses and reading circles.

During the current year the series will consist of five "double numbers" of 32 pages or more, each. The separate numbers will be edited respectively by Dana Carleton Munro, A.M. and Edith Bramhall, A.M., of the University of Pennsylvania, Edwin Knox Mitchell, of Hartford Theological Seminary, Edward P. Cheyney, A.M., of the University of Pennsylvania, Arthur C. Howland, Ph. D., of the University of Illinois, and Merrick Whitcomb, Ph.D., of the University of Pennsylvania. Titles of the numbers and further particulars are given on the third cover page.

TRANSLATIONS AND REPRINTS
FROM THE
ORIGINAL SOURCES OF EUROPEAN HISTORY.

Vol. IV.   Documents Illustrative of Feudalism.   No. 3

TABLE OF CONTENTS.

PART I. THE ORIGINS OF FEUDALISM, A. D., 500–1100.

			PAGE
I.		PERSONAL DEPENDENCE.	
	1.	An Anglo-Saxon Formula of Commendation,	3
	2.	A Frankish Formula of Commendation,	3
	3.	Acceptance of an Antrustion,	4
	4.	A Charter of Guardianship,	4
	5.	Capitulary concerning Freemen and Vassals	5
	6.	Capitulary of Mersen,	5
	7.	Commendation, from Domesday Book,	5
II.		DEPENDENT LAND TENURE.	
	1.	Gift and Return as a Precaria,	6
	2.	Grants of Bishop Oswald,	8
	3.	Change from Allodial to Feudal Holding,	10
III.		PRIVATE JURISDICTIONS.	
	1.	Immunity for Lands of a Bishopric,	11
	2.	Immunity to a Layman,	12
	3.	Anglo-Saxon Grant of Immunity	13
	4.	Capitulary of Kiersey,	14

PART II. FEUDAL INSTITUTIONS, A. D., 1100–1400.

I.		GRANTS AND ACKNOWLEDGMENTS OF FIEFS.	
	1.	Acknowledgment of Feudal Tenure,	15
	2.	Grant of a Fief, A. D. 1210,	15
	3.	Grant of a Fief, A. D. 1167,	15
	4.	Feudal Holdings,	16
	5.	Grant of a Fief of Money,	17
II.		CEREMONY OF HOMAGE AND FEALTY.	
	1.	Count of Flanders,	18
	2.	Homage and Fealty of Bernard Atton,	18
	3.	Legal Rules for Homage and Fealty,	20
III.		SUBINFEUDATION.	
	1.	From the Exchequer Rolls,	21
	2.	From the Hundred Rolls,	22
IV.		GENERAL DUTIES OF LORDS AND VASSALS.	
	1.	Letter from Bishop Fulbert,	23
	2.	From an English Code,	24
V.		AUTHORITY OF LORD OVER MARRIAGES.	
	1.	Acknowledgment of Countess of Nevers,	24
	2.	From Chronicle of Lambert,	25
	3.	Fees for License to Marry,	25

TABLE OF CONTENTS CONTINUED.

		PAGE
VI.	WARDSHIP, RELIEF AND AIDS.	
	1. Wardship, from the Exchequer Rolls,	26
	2. Relief, from the Exchequer Rolls,	27
	3. Acknowledgment of Relief,	27
	4. Three familiar Aids,	28
VII.	MILITARY SERVICE.	
	1. An Early Summons,	28
	2. Grant to a Knight,	29
	3. Service, according to the Hundred Rolls,	29
	4. Acknowledgment of Military Duty,	29
	5. Legal Rules for Service,	30
	6. Instance of Count of Champagne,	30
	7. Answers of Tenants to Summons,	31
VIII.	FEUDAL JUSTICE.	
	1. English Customs,	32
	2. Royal Writ to Secure Jurisdiction,	33
	3. Legal Rules for Trial,	33
	4. Instance of Condemnation,	33
IX.	RIGHT OF COINAGE.	
	1. Grant of the Mint,	34
	2. Promise of Restriction,	35
X.	FORFEITURE.	

I. THE ORIGINS OF FEUDALISM, A.D. 500-1100.

Feudalism is the name given to that form and degree of organization and system in European society which existed at a period when there were no strong central governments, when there was no civil equality of persons, and no conception of absolute property in land. The absence of these institutions was more or less characteristic of all the countries of western Europe from the ninth to the fourteenth century. Any effort to illustrate such a condition of society by contemporary documents is necessarily somewhat fallacious, for Europe was above all else disorganized and anarchic, while formal documents always give an impression of order and regularity.

On the other hand such a mere dominion of force as has been spoken of, which certainly tended to exist when the more orderly conditions of the period of the Roman Empire and of the early barbarian monarchies had passed away, was limited in several respects. It was modified notably by personal alliances of lord and vassal, by praedial relations of landlord and tenant, by the exercise of many of the powers of government on their own lands by nobles one or more stages below the national ruler. A vast number of documents, edicts, formulas, and contemporary records illustrate this side of the growth of Feudalism. These documents show that from an early period both among the Romans and the barbarians a habit of forming voluntary personal agreements of protection on the one hand and service on the other between a superior and an inferior was prevalent; secondly, that the definiteness of the legal Roman idea of private ownership of land was becoming blunted, and the communal idea of its ownership by the clan was being lost, so that they were both superseded by an ideal of beneficiary or undefined land holding, which was quite satisfied with the profitable superiority over the land by its lord and the practical use of it by its ultimate tenant, without raising the question of its actual ownership; and thirdly, that the power of local nobles and the connivance of the weak central government combined to place military, judicial, and even certain legislative and administrative powers in the hands of those whose only claim to them was that they were lords over vassals and holders of lands.

The documents in Part I, are intended to illustrate these three customs, which are commonly known respectively as commendation, the creation of beneficies, and the grant of immunities.

I. THE GROWTH OF PERSONAL DEPENDENCE.

1. AN ANGLO-SAXON FORMULA OF COMMENDATION.

Schmidt: Gesetze der Angelsachsen, p. 404.   Anglo-Saxon.

Thus shall one take the oath of fidelity:

By the Lord before whom this sanctuary is holy, I will to N. be true and faithful, and love all which he loves and shun all which he shuns, according to the laws of God and the order of the world. Nor will I ever with will or action, through word or deed, do anything which is unpleasing to him, on condition that he will hold to me as I shall deserve it, and that he will perform everything as it was in our agreement when I submitted myself to him and chose his will.

2. A FRANKISH FORMULA OF COMMENDATION, SEVENTH CENTURY.

Rozière: Collection de Formules, No. XLIII, Vol. I, p. 69.   Latin.

Who commends himself in the power of another:

To that magnificent lord *so and so*, I, *so and so*. Since it is known familiarly to all how little I have whence to feed and clothe myself, I have therefore petitioned your piety, and your good-will has decreed to me that I should hand myself over or commend myself to your guardianship, which I have thereupon done; that is to say in this way, that you should aid and succor me as well with food as with clothing, according as I shall be able to serve you and deserve it.

And so long as I shall live I ought to provide service and honor to you, suitably to my free condition; and I shall not during the time of my life have the ability to withdraw from your power or guardianship; but must remain during the days of my life under your power or defence. Wherefore it is proper that if either of us shall wish to wit draw himself from these agreements, he shall pay *so many* shillings to his peer (*pari suo*) and this agreement shall remain unbroken.

Wherefore it is fitting that they should make or confirm between themselves two letters drawn up in the same form on this matter; which they have thus done.

3. ACCEPTANCE OF AN ANTRUSTION, SEVENTH CENTURY.

Rozière: Collection de Formules, No. VIII, Vol. I, p. 8. Latin.

It is right that those who offer to us unbroken fidelity should be protected by our aid. And since *such and such* a faithful one of ours, by the favor of God, coming here in our palace with his arms, has seen fit to swear trust and fidelity to us in our hand, therefore we decree and command by the present precept that for the future *such and such* above mentioned be counted with the number of the antrustions. And if anyone perchance should presume to kill him, let him know that he will be judged guilty of his wergild of 600 shillings.

4. CHARTER OF GUARDIANSHIP GRANTED BY THE KING. NINTH CENTURY.

Rozière: Collection de Formules, No. XIII, Vol. I, p. 14. Latin.

We wish it to be known to all our faithful, dwelling in the parts of Romania and Italy that certain men whose names are *such and such*, coming into our presence have begged and prayed us that on account of the injuries of evil men we should take them under the security of our protection, which we have done with willingness. On this account we have ordered this precept of our authority to be made and given to them; by which we require and command that no one of you take anything of their property from them against what is right, or presume to prosecute them in any cause unjustly; but it is allowed to them under our defence and protection and without opposition of any kind to live quietly on their own property. And if any causes shall have arisen against them which within their own country cannot be concluded without heavy and unreasonable expense, we will that these be suspended and reserved for our presence till they may receive a just and lawful final sentence, and let no one presume to deprive them of the opportunity of coming to us.

5. CAPITULARY CONCERNING FREEMEN AND VASSALS, A. D. 816.

M. G. LL, I, 196. Latin.

If anyone shall wish to leave his lord (*seniorem*,) and is able to prove against him one of these crimes, that is, in the first place, if the lord has wished to reduce him unjustly into servitude; in the second place, if he has taken counsel against his life; in the third place if the lord has committed adultery with the wife of his vassal, in the fourth place if he has wilfully attacked him with a drawn sword; in the fifth place, if the lord has been able to bring defence to his vassal after he has commended his hands to him, and has not done so; it is allowed to the vassal to leave him. If the lord has perpetrated anything against the vassal in these five points it is allowed the vassal to leave him.

6. CAPITULARY OF MERSEN, A. D. 847.

M. G. LL. I, 395. Latin.

We will moreover that each free man in our kingdom shall choose a lord, from us or our faithful, such a one as he wishes.

We command moreover that no man shall leave his lord without just cause, nor should any one receive him, except in such a way as was customary in the time of our predecessors.

And we wish you to know that we want to grant right to our faithful subjects and we do not wish to do anything to them against reason. Similarly we admonish you and the rest of our faithful subjects that you grant right to your men and do not act against reason toward them.

And we will that the man of each one of us[1] in whosoever kingdom he is, shall go with his lord against the enemy, or in his other needs unless there shall have been (as may there not be) such an invasion of the kingdom as is called a *landwer*, so that the whole people of that kingdom shall go together to repel it.

7. INSTANCES OF COMMENDATION FROM DOMESDAY BOOK, A. D. 1085.

The reference to most of these passages is due to Prof. F. W. Maitland, whose "*Domesday Book and Beyond*," has entirely transformed the study of early English Feudalism, as of so many other elements of English mediæval history. The same remark applies to Oswald's Grants, Document II, 2, p. 8.

---

[1] i. e. Lothar, Lewis and Charles.

In Greenwich were two free men, one commended to King Edward, the other to Girth.

Suffolk, i, 347.

In the borough[1] Roger has thirty-three men commended to him whom his predecessor held, in whom he had nothing except commendation.

Norfolk, i, 173.

In Wantage hundred the same bishop holds from the king one hide and a half, and Tori from him. The father of Tori held it in the time of King Edward, and was able to go whither he wished, but for his protection he committed himself to bishop Herman, and Tori similarly to bishop Osmund.

Berkshire, i, 58.

This land Edmund, a man of Earl Harold, held.

Hertfordshire, i, 133.

In Munehale a certain Englishman holds from Geoffrey three virgates, which he held as a free man in the time of King Edward; and in the time of King William he became the man of Geoffrey, of his own free will.

Essex, i, 62 b.

In Becham one free man holds by commendation from bishop Almar 80 acres of land.

Norfolk, i, 198 b.

In the borough there were 943 burghers in the time of King Edward. Of these the king has the whole custom. Of these men there were 36 so completely in the domain of King Edward that they were not able to be the men of any one without the license of the king. All the rest were able to be the men of any one, but the custom nevertheless remained to the king, except heriot.

Thetford, Norfolk, i, 186 b.

II. THE GROWTH OF DEPENDENT LAND TENURE.

1. GRANT OF LANDS TO A MONASTERY, AND THEIR RETURN AS A PRECARIA, SEVENTH CENTURY.

Rozière : Collection de Formules, No. CCCL, Vol. I, p. 433. Latin.

I, *such a one*, in the name of God. I have settled in my mind that

---

[1] Thetford.

I ought, for the good of my soul, to make a gift of something from my possessions, which I have therefore done. And this is what I hand over, in the district named *so and so*, in the place of which the name is *such and such*, all those possessions of mine which there my father left me at his death, and which as against my brothers or as against my coheirs the lot legitimately brought me in the division; or those which I was able afterward to add to them in any way, in their whole completeness, that is to say the courtyard with its buildings, with slaves, houses, lands cultivated and uncultivated, meadows, woods, waters, mills, etc. These, as I have before said, with all the things adjacent or appurtenant to them I hand over to the church, which was built in honor of *such and such a saint* to the monastery which is called *so and so*, where *such and such* an abbott is acknowledged to rule regularly over God's flock; on these conditions, viz: That so long as life remains in my body, the possessions above described I shall receive from you as a benefice for usufruct, and the due payment I will make to you and your successors each year, that is *so and so much*. And my son shall have the same possessions for the days of his life only, and shall make the above named payment; and if my children should survive me they shall have the same possessions during the days of their life and shall make the same payment; and if God shall give me a son from a legitimate wife, he shall have the same possessions for the days of his life only, after the death of whom the same possessions with all their improvements shall return to your part to be held forever; and if it should be my chance to beget sons from a legitimate marriage, these shall hold the same possessions after my death, making the above named payment, during the time of their lives. If not, however, after my death, without tergiversation of any kind, by right of your authority, the same possessions shall revert to you to be retained forever. If any one, however, which I do not believe will ever occur, if I myself or any other person shall wish to violate the firmness and validity of this grant, the order of truth opposing him, may his falsity in no degree succeed; and for his bold attempt may he pay to the aforesaid monastery double the amount which his ill-ordered cupidity has been prevented from abstracting; and moreover let him be culpable to the royal authority for *such and such an amount* of gold; and, nevertheless, let the present charter remain inviolate with all that it contains, with the witnesses placed below.

Done in *such and such* a place, publicly, those who are noted below being present, or the remaining innumerable multitude of people.

In the name of God, I, abbott *so and so*, with our commissioned brethren. Since it is not unknown how you, *such and such a one*, by the suggestion of divine exhortation did grant to *such and such* a monastery, to the church which is known to be constructed in honor of *such and such a saint*, where we by God's authority exercise our pastoral care, all your possessions which you seemed to have in the district named, in the vill named, which your father on his death bequeathed to you there, or which by your own labor you were able to gain there, or which as against your brother or against *such and such* a co-heir, a just division gave you, with courtyard and buildings, gardens and orchards, with various slaves, *so and so* by name, houses, lands, meadows, woods, cultivated and uncultivated, or with all the dependencies and appurtenances belonging to it, which it would be extremely long to enumerate, in all their completeness; but afterwards, at your request, it has seemed proper to us to cede to you the same possessions to be held for usufruct; and you will not neglect to pay at annual periods the due *censum* hence, that is *so and so much*. And if God should give you a son by your legal wife, he shall have the same possessions for the days of his life only, and shall not presume to neglect the above named payment, and similarly your sons which you are seen to have at present, shall do for the days of their life; after the death of whom all the possessions above named shall revert to us and our successors perpetually. Moreover, if no sons shall have been begotten by you, immediately after your death, without any prejudicial contention, they shall revert to the rulers or guardians of the above named church, forever, Nor may any one, either ourselves or our successors, be successful in a rash attempt inordinately to destroy these agreements, but just as the time has demanded in the present *precaria*, may that be sure to endure unchanged which we, with the consent of our brothers, have decided to corroborate.

Done *in such and such a place*, in the presence of *so and so* and of others whom it is not worth while to enumerate. Seal of the same abbott, who has ordered this *precaria* to be made.

2. OSWALD'S GRANTS OF SUBJECT-LANDS, A. D., 970.
Kemble: Saxons in England, I, 517-19. Latin.

To my dearest lord Edgar, King of the English, I, Oswald, bishop of the church of Worcester, return thanks before God and men for all the gifts which by your clemency have been granted to me. Therefore, if the mercy of God will allow, before God and men will I always remain faithful to you, remembering in my gratitude your abundant goodness, in granting to me that which I desired so deeply, and taking up my quarrel and that of the holy church of God. This you did through the aid and intervention of my spokesmen, the most reverend archbishop Dunstan, and the venerable Aethelwold, bishop of Winchester, and that magnificent man, Earl Brihtnoth; and in accordance with the counsel of his wise men and magnates decided it justly, and to the sustentation of the church which he graciously committed to me to rule. Wherefore, in what manner with the lands which were handed over to my power, I have endowed my dependents, for the space of life of three men, that is of two heirs after themselves, with the license and attestation of the same my lord king, it has pleased both myself and my helpers and counsellors to explain openly through the form of a chirograph to my brethren and successors, that is the bishops. They will thus know what ought justly to be required from them according to the agreement made with them and with their promise. I have also been careful to compose this letter by way of caution, lest any one in the future, instigated by wicked cupidity, and desiring to change this, should renounce the service of the church. So this agreement was made with them, the same my lord king approving and by his attestation corroborating and confirming the greatness of his munificence, all the wise men and magnates of his court attesting and consenting.

With this agreement I have conceded to them the lands of holy church to be held under me, that is that all the law of riding which pertains to *equites* should be fulfilled by them; and that they should fully perform all those things which justly belong to the right of the same church, that is to say those things which in English are called churchscot and toll (that is *theloneum*), and tac (that is *swinsceade*,) and other rights of the church, unless the bishop shall wish to pardon anything to any one of them; and they must, moreover, affirm with an oath that so long as they hold his lands they will continue humbly in all subjection to the commands of the bishop. Besides this, moreover, they shall provide themselves ready for every need of the bishop; they shall provide horses, they themselves shall ride; and for all the burning of lime for the need of the church and for the building of the bridge they shall be found ready; moreover they shall provide, of their own accord, for building the hunting lodge of the lord bishop, and shall turn their own spears to hunting whenever it shall please the lord bishop. Moreove for the many other occasions of need which the lord bishop often requires, either for his own service or to fulfill that to the king, they should always be subjected in all humility to the governance of that leader and to the will of whomsoever presides over the episcopal office, on account of the benefices which have been granted to them, according to his will and according to the quantity of lands which each one possesses.

When the aforesaid course of time shall have passed away, that is to say, the period of life of two heirs after those who now possess them, it shall rest with the judgment of the same bishop as to what he wishes, and whatever his will is, so it shall stand, either to retain these to his own need, if so he shall judge it is useful to him, or to grant them for a longer time to any one if it shall so seem good to him, so, nevertheless, that the service of the church shall always, as we have said above, be fully provided for.

But if any of those rights mentioned above shall have failed because of the crime of any one misrepresenting, let him atone for the crime of his misrepresentation according to the right of the bishop, or let him be deprived of that gift and land which he before had control of. If there should be any one, tempted by the devil, (as we should hope not) who, by means of our benefice, should attempt by fraud to deprive the church of God, either of its property or of its due service, let him be deprived of our benediction and of all blessing of God and his saints, unless by the most profound repentance, he hastens to correct it and restores to its original condition what he has defrauded it of; for it is written: "robbers and sacrilegious men shall not reach the kingdom of God." Now, however, for the sake of God and Holy Mary, in whose name this monastery is endowed, I advise and require that in no way should any one venture to wrest this, but as by us it has been established, as we have described above, so let it remain forever. He who keeps this let him be filled with all benediction; he, however, who infringes it let him be cursed by the Lord and all saints, Amen.

3. CHANGE FROM ALLODIAL TO FEUDAL HOLDING.

Quantin: Recueil de Pièces du XIII Siècle, No. 631, pp. 310-11. Latin.

This instance of the original entrance of a piece of land into feudal relations, is of course at a date centuries after feudal tenure had become characteristic of most of the land of Europe, but it seems to be typical of conditions even at this late period, in the south of France. See discussion in Luchaire and in Boutaric.

To all who shall see the present letters, the Official of Auxerre, greeting. Let all know, that standing in presence William de la Forêt, knight, and Agnes, his wife, asserting firmly that they hold and possess in free allod the property noted below; viz: the arpent of vines, situated in the vineyard of Chablis, in the place which is called the Close, between the vines of William Berner, on the one side and the vines of the late Pariot, on the other, [1]. . . . . . . also all other things which they possessed and held in free allod, as they said, and still hold and possess within the boundaries of Chablis, of Chichiac, of Milli, of Ponche, of Bena and of Chapelle, the direct and hereditary holdings of the same Agnes wherever they may be within the same boundaries, and whatsoever; by their common consent and will, after previous deliberation they have placed altogether in the fee of the church of St. Martin of Tours, and in fee, for the future have wished to hold and possess firmly from the said church.

They promise, on their fealty offered by their bodies, that they hold and will hold the things aforesaid and expressed above, with all other things which they hold and possess within the said boundaries wherever they may be and whatsoever, for the future, from the said church in fee, and to the same church in future, by reason of the same property will provide feudal service as they ought to provide it, just as others holding in fee are accustomed to hold and are bound to give or provide.

Given A. D. 1267, Wednesday after the Ascension of the Lord.

III. PRIVATE JURISDICTIONS.

1. GRANT OF IMMUNITY FOR THE LANDS OF A BISHOPRIC.

Rozière : Recueil de Formules, No. XVI, Vol. I, p. 17. Latin.

We believe that it increases the great memorial of our realm, if with benevolent deliberation we concede opportune benefits to the places of the churches or to *any one you may name*, and under the protection of the Lord, write them down to endure in stability. Therefore, may your zeal know that we have seen fit upon petition to grant such a benefit, for our eternal reward, to that apostolic man, lord *so and so*, bishop of *such and such a city;* that in the villa of the church of that lord, which in recent times, or in ours, or by the gift of any one, he is seen to have, or which in the future godly piety shall wish to amplify in the right of that holy place, no public judge shall at any time presume to enter for the hearing of causes or for the exaction of payments, but the prelate himself or his successors for the name of the Lord shall be able to rule over this under the name of a complete corporation. We require, therefore, that neither you nor your subordinates nor your successors nor any public judicial power should presume at any time to enter into the vills of the same church anywhere in our kingdom, either those granted by royal bounty or by that of private persons or those which shall in future be granted; either for the sake of hearing altercations or to exact fines for any causes, or to obtain sureties. But whatever the Treasury could expect either of fines or other things either from freemen or from servants and other nations who are within the fields or boundaries or dwelling upon the lands of the aforesaid church; by our indulgence for our future welfare, shall be profitable for the expenses of the same church by the hand of those ruling it, forever. And what we for the name of God and the remedy of our soul and that of our progeny who shall follow us have granted from full devotion, let not the royal sublimity, in the reckless cupidity of any of the judges be tempted to break. And, in order that the present authority may, by the aid of God, remain inviolate in present as in future times we have ordered this to be corroborated below by the subscription of our hand.

2. GRANT OF IMMUNITY TO A LAYMAN, SEVENTH CENTURY.

Rozière: Recueil de Formules, No. CXLVII. Vol. I, p. 185., Latin.

Therefore, may your greatness or perseverance know that we have seen fit to concede by our ready will to *such and such an* illustrious man, the vill named *so and so*, situated in *such and such* a district, completely with its whole proper boundary, as it has been possessed by *such and such a one* or by our treasury, or is possessed at this present time. Wherefore, by our present authority we have decreed what we command shall be kept forever, that the man aforesaid, *so and so*, should have conceded to him *such and such* a vill as we have said, in its entirety, with the lands, houses, buildings, villeins, slaves, vineyards, woods, fields, meadows, pastures, waters or watercourses, grist mills, additions, appurtenances, or any kind of men who are subjected to our treasury who dwell there; in entire immunity, and without the entrance of any one of the judges for the purpose of holding the pleas of any kind of causes. Thus he may have, hold, and possess it in proprietary right and without expecting the entrance of any of the judges; and may leave the possession of it to his posterity, by the aid of God, from our bounty, or to whom he will; and by our permission he shall have free power to do whatever he may wish with it for the future. And in order that this authority may be held as more firm, we have decreed it to be corroborated below with our own hand.

3. ANGLO-SAXON GRANT OF IMMUNITY, A. D., 1053.

Thorpe: Diplomatarium Anglicum, p. 368. Anglo-Saxon.

Such grants as the following have not usually been recognized as grants of immunity, and our ignorance as to the exact significance of the Anglo-Saxon technical terms employed makes it impossible to decide the extent of the exemptions granted. But there seems to be no doubt that the result of such a grant was to give the recipients the right to all the profits of justice, and exemption from the intrusion of royal officials, and therefore inferentially the right and duty of holding courts and exercising other forms of jurisdiction. See Maitland: "*Domesday Book and Beyond,*" especially Essay II, sect. 3.

I, King Edward, greet bishop Wulfwig and earl Gyrth and all my thanes in Oxfordshire amicably, and I make known to you that I have given to Christ and Saint Peter in Westminster, the village in which I was born, by name Islip, and a half-hide at Marsh, scot-free and rent free, with all the things which thereto belong, in wood and in field, in mead and in water, with church and with church socn, as full and as complete and as free as it stood in my own hand, and as Aelfgifu Emma, my mother, gave it to me at my birthday, as a first gift, and naturally bequeathed it. And I give them, moreover, sac and socn, toll and team, and infangenethe of and bloodwite and wardwite and hamsocn, and foresteal, grithbryce and mundbryce, and all the rights which to me belong. I now greet well my beloved kinsman at Wallingford, and I enjoin thee that thou in my stead deliver that land into the possession of the saint, for I will on no account allow that any man have any authority there, in any thing or at any times, except the abbot and the brethren, for the monastery's necessary requirements. And whoso shall faithfully hold this alms may God and God's mother hold him in everlasting bliss. And whoso shall turn it aside, be he turned aside from God to the rigid tortures of hell's inmates, unless he in this earth the more rigidly make amends. God and St. Peter's favor pre-

4. FROM THE CAPITULARY OF KIERSEY, A. D., 877.
M. G., LL., Vol. I, p. 542. Latin.

If a count of this kingdom, whose son is with us, shall die, our son with the rest of our faithful shall appoint some one of the nearest relatives of the same count, who, along with the officials of his province and with the bishop in whose diocese the same province is, shall administer that province until announcement is made to us, so that we may honor his son who is with us with his honors.

If, however, he had a minor son, this same son, along with the officials of that province and with the bishop in whose diocese it is, shall make provision for the same province until the notice of the death of the same count shall come to us, that his son may be honored, by our concession, with his honors.

If, however, he had no son, our son along with the rest of the faithful, shall take charge, who, along with the officials of the same province and with the proper bishop shall make provision for the same province until our order may be made in regard to it. Therefore, let him not be angry who shall provide for the province if we give the same province to another whom it pleases us, rather than to him who has so far provided for it.

Similarly also shall this be done concerning our vassals. And we will and command that as well the bishops as the abbots and the counts, and any others of our faithful also, shall study to preserve this toward their men.

II. FEUDAL INSTITUTIONS, A. D. 1100-1400.

The relation of lord and vassal, the engagements between lord and tenant, and the feudal possession of political powers, as time passed on, obtained a greater amount of fixedness and uniformity. That is to say, there came to be well-defined feudal institutions in existence. Moreover, in local tradition, in documentary formulas, in charters issued by kings or great feudal lords, and finally in legal treatises, such as the *Coutumiers* of various French provinces, the *Sachsenspiegel*, or the *Libri Feudorum*, there grew up a body of established feudal law or custom which could be appealed to as authoritative. Thus by the thirteenth century Feudalism, as far as it extended, was a tolerably regular system. But by this time also many non-feudal influences were already growing in strength. The centralized monarchies, city life, the system of national estates, commerce, manufactures, money capital, were increasing in influence while feudal institutions were both absolutely and relatively losing in importance. Feudalism therefore merely bridges over the chasm lying between one set of orderly institutions, those of the

Roman Empire and the early barbarian monarchies, and another, those of the reviving national monarchies of the thirteenth and subsequent centuries. The documents in Part II are intended to illustrate feudal institutions as they took shape in the twelfth and thirteenth centuries.

I. GRANTS AND ACKNOWLEDGMENTS OF FIEFS.

1. ACKNOWLEDGMENT OF FEUDAL TENURE, A. D. 1220.

Quantin, Recueil de Pièces du XIII Siècle No. 264, p. 116. Latin.

I, Guy, lord of Maligny, make known to all who shall see this present letter that I hold from the count of Champagne, the chateau of Maligny, and the manors which are subject to the jurisdiction of and liable to revert to the same count at small and great force, and the knights' fees which are held from Maligny, and whatever I have at La Chapelle, near Maligny, and whatever I have at Beine, except Henry and his family, and Sir Guy of Montreal, and whatever I have at Chablis, which is in the name of my wife. And that this may be known for the future I have strengthened the present letter with the support of my seal. Given in the year of grace 1220, in the month of February.

2. GRANT OF A FIEF, A. D., 1200.

Quantin: Recueil de Pièces du XIII Siècle, No. 2. Latin.

I, Thiebault, count palatine of Troyes, make known to those present and to come that I have given in fee to Jocelyn d'Avalon and his heirs the manor which is called Gillencourt, which is of the castellanerie of La Ferte sur Aube; and whatever the same Jocelyn shall be able to acquire in the same manor I have granted to him and his heirs in augmentation of that fief, I have granted, moreover, to him that in no free manor of mine will I retain men who are of this gift. The same Jocelyn, moreover, on account of this has become my liege man, saving however, his allegiance to Gerard d'Arcy, and to the lord duke of Burgundy, and to Peter, count of Auxerre. Done at Chouaude, by my own witness, in the year of the Incarnation of our Lord 1200 in the month of January. Given by the hand of Walter, my chancellor; note of Milo.

3. GRANT OF A FIEF, A. D., 1167.

Brussel: Usage des Fiefs, I, 3, note. Latin.

In the name of the Holy and Undivided Trinity, Amen. I, Louis, by the grace of God, king of the French, make known to all present as well as to come, that at Mante in our presence, Count Henry of Champagne conceded the fief of Savigny to Bartholomew, bishop of Beauvais, and his successors. And for that fief the said bishop has made promise and engagement for one knight and justice and service to Count Henry; and he has also agreed that the bishops who shall come after him will do likewise. In order that this may be understood and known to posterity we have caused the present charter to be corroborated by our seal; done at Mante, in the year of the Incarnate Word 1167; present in our palace those whose names and seals are appended: seal of count Thiebault, our steward; seal of Guy, the butler; seal of Matthew, the chamberlain; seal of Ralph, the constable. Given by the hand of Hugh, the chancellor.

4. FEUDAL HOLDINGS IN ENGLAND, A. D. 1166.

Red Book of the Exchequer, Rolls Series, Vol. I, pp. 246, 342, 312, 313. Latin.

In 1166 an order seems to have been sent out from the royal Exchequer in England requiring all tenants-in-chief to make formal report to the king of the number and names of the subtenants who had been enfeoffed on their lands previous to 1135, of those subsequently, and of the number they owed to the king from their lands in addition to these military subtenants. The returns to this summons, which give exceedingly valuable information for the military side of feudalism, are preserved in the "Red Book of the Exchequer," lately published in the Rolls Series, a i .nterpreted by Mr. J. H. Round in his work entitled *"Feudal England,"* especially pp. 236 ff.

To his dearest lord Henry, by the grace of God king of the English, William of London, greeting:

Know that I have no knight enfeoffed of old or recently, but I ought to defend my fief with the service of my body.

To Henry, by the grace of God king of the English, Peter de Mare, greeting:

Let it be known to you that I hold Lavington, by your grace, in domain, for the service of two knights. But I have no knight enfeoffed there, either by old or recent feoffment.

To Henry, king of the English, duke of the Normans and Aquitanians, and count of the Angevins, Roger de Burun, greeting:

Concerning my knights in the time of king Henry, know this to be true: W. de Heriz holds two knights' fees; Roger de Cordingestoke two knights' fees; Patrick de Rosel, one knights' fee; and Albert, whom my father enfeoffed after the death of king Henry, one knights' fee. And I myself fulfill the service of four knights from my domain.

Earl Walter Giffard[1] had these knights enfeoffed in old feoffment; Hugh Bolebeche owed the earl the service of twenty knights; Geoffrey Fitz-William, of twenty-seven knights; Manasser Bisset, of one knight; William de Saukeville, of one knight; Hugh de Noers, of one knight; Gerard de Granville, of three knights; Wido de Rocheford, of three knights; Richard Talbot, of two knights; William Passeleue, of three knights; William Buteri, of five knights; Peter Corbuzone, of five knights; Richard Fitz-Mabel, of four knights; Gerard de Reddenham, of two knights; Walter de Weston, of two knights; Jordan de Belnair, of two knights; Pagan de Dertone, of one knight; Henry de Oyli, of one knight; Hugh de Cresi, of one knight; Elias Giffard, of two knights. Robert de Neville, of one knight; Ralph de Lucintou, of one knight; Matilda de Bec, of one knight; the son of William Fitz-Roger, of one knight; Hamo Fitz-Bener, of half a knight; Roger de St. Faith, of half a knight; Robert de Bedford, of half a knight; Sawalle de Crendon, of half a knight, supported by the earl; Gerard de Bodingham, of half a knight; Alan de Bodingham, of half a knight; Adam de St. Lawrence, of half a knight: Richar de Witewelle, of half a knight; Richard Makerel, of half a knight. Of recent feoffment, Hugh de Millville has the fee of half a knight; William Cokerel, of half a knight; William de Bureville, of half a knight.

5. GRANT OF A FIEF OF MONEY, A. D., 1380.
Boutaric; Institutions Militaires de la France, p. 121. Latin.

We, Regnault de Fauquemont, knight, lord of Bournes and of Sitter, make known to all by these presents, that we have become liege man of the king of France, our lord, and to him have made faith and homage because of 1000 livres of Tours of income which he has given to us during our life, to be drawn from his treasury at Paris. And we have promised to him and do promise by these presents to serve him loyally and well in his wars and otherwise against all who can live and die, in the form and manner in which a good and loyal subject ought to serve his sovereign lord. In testimony of which we have put our seal to these present letters. Given at Paris, the 15th day of June, the year 1380.

II. THE CEREMONY OF HOMAGE AND FEALTY.

1. HOMAGE AND FEALTY TO COUNT OF FLANDERS, A. D., 1127.

Galbert de Bruges, Chronicle of the Death of Charles the Good,
Ed. by Pirenne, p. 89. Latin.

Through the whole remaining part of the day those who had been previously enfeoffed by the most pious count Charles, did homage to the count, taking up now again their fiefs and offices and whatever they had before rightfully and legitimately obtained. On Thursday the seventh of April, homages were again made to the count being completed in the following order of faith and security.

First they did their homage thus, the count asked if he was willing to become completely his man, and the other replied, "I am willing"; and with clasped hands, surrounded by the hands of the count, they were bound together by a kiss. Secondly, he who had done homage gave his fealty to the representative of the count in these words, "I promise on my faith that I will in future be faithful to count William, and will observe my homage to him completely against all persons in good faith and without deceit," and thirdly, he took his oath to this upon the relics of the saints. Afterward, with a little rod which the count held in his hand, he gave investitures to all who by this agreement had given their security and homage and accompanying oath.

2. CHARTER OF HOMAGE AND FEALTY, A. D., 1110.

Teulet: Layettes du Trésor des Chartes, No., 39, Vol. I, p. 36. Latin.

In the name of the Lord, I, Bernard Atton, Viscount of Carcassonne, in the presence of my sons, Roger and Trencavel, and of Peter Roger of Barbazan, and William Hugo, and Raymond Mantellini, and Peter de Vietry, nobles, and of many other honorable men, who had come to the monastery of St. Mary of Grasse, to the honor of the festival of the august St. Mary; since lord Leo, abbot of the said monastery, has asked me, in the presence of all those above mentioned, to acknowledge to him the fealty and homage for the castles, manors, and places which the patrons, my ancestors, held from him and his predecessors and from the said monastery as a fief, and which I ought to hold as they held, I have made to the lord abbot Leo acknowledgment and homage as I ought to do.

Therefore, let all present and to come know that I the said Bernard Atton, lord and viscount of Carcassonne, acknowledge verily to thee my lord Leo, by the grace of God, abbot of St. Mary of Grasse, and to thy successors that I hold and ought to hold as a fief, in Carcassonne, the following: that is to say, the castles of Confoles, of Leocque, of Capendes, (which is otherwise known as St. Martin of Sussagues); and the manors of Mairac, of Albars and of Musso; also, in the valley of Aquitaine, Rieux, Traverina, Hérault, Archas, Servians, Villatritoes, Tansiraus, Presler, Cornelles. Moreover, I acknowledge that I hold from thee and from the said monastery as a fief the castle of Termes in Narbonne; and in Minerve the castle of Ventaion, and the manors of Cassanolles, and of Ferral and Aiohars; and in Le Rogès, the little village of Longville; for each and all of which I make homage and fealty with hands and with mouth to thee my said lord abbot Leo and to thy successors, and I swear upon these four gospels of God that I will always be a faithful vassal to thee and to thy successors and to St. Mary of Grasse in all things in which a vassal is required to be faithful to his lord, and I will defend thee, my lord, and all thy successors, and the said monastery and the monks present and to come and the castles and manors and all your men and their possessions against all malefactors and invaders, at my request and that of my successors at my own cost; and I will give to thee power over all the castles and manors above described, in peace and in war, whenever they shall be claimed by thee or by thy successors.

Moreover I acknowledge that, as a recognition of the above fiefs, I and my successors ought to come to the said monastery, at our own expense, as often as a new abbot shall have been made, and there do homage and return to him the power over all the fiefs described above. And when the abbot shall mount his horse I and my heirs, viscounts of Carcassonne, and our successors ought to hold the stirrup for the honor of the dominion of St. Mary of Grasse; and to him and all who come with him, to as many as two hundred beasts, we should make the abbot's purveyance in the borough of St. Michael of Carcassonne, the first time he enters Carcassonne, with the best fish and meat and with eggs and cheese, honorably according to his will, and pay the expense of the shoeing of the horses, and for straw and fodder as the season shall require.

And if I or my sons or their successors do not observe to thee or to thy successors each and all the things declared above, and should come against these things, we wish that all the aforesaid fiefs should by that very fact be handed over to thee and to the said monastery of St. Mary of Grasse and to thy successors.

I, therefore, the aforesaid lord Leo, by the grace of God, abbot of St. Mary of Grasse, receive the homage and fealty for all the fiefs of castles and manors and places which are described above; in the way and with the agreements and understandings written above ; and likewise I concede to thee and thy heirs and their successors, the viscounts of Carcassonne, all the castles and manors and places aforesaid, as a fief, along with this present charter, divided through the alphabet. And I promise to thee and thy heirs and successors, viscounts of Carcassonne, under the religion of my order, that I will be good and faithful lord concerning all those things described above.

Moreover, I, the aforesaid viscount, acknowledge that the little villages of Cannetis, Maironis, Villamagna, Aiglino, Villadasas, Villafrancos, Villadenz, Villaudriz, St. Genése, Gauart, Conguste and Mata, with the farm-house of Mathus and the chateaux of Villalauro and Claromont, with the little villages of St. Stephen of Surlac, and of Upper and Lower Agrifolio, ought to belong to the said monastery, and whoever holds anything there holds from the same monastery, as we have seen and have heard read in the privileges and charters of the monastery, and as was there written.

Made in the year of the Incarnation of the Lord 1110, in the reign of Louis. Seal of Bernard Atton, viscount of Carcassonne, seal of Raymond Mantellini, seal of Peter Roger of Barbazon, seal of Roger, son of the said viscount of Carcassonne, seal of Peter de Vitry, seal of Trencavel, son of the said viscount of Carcassonne, seal of William Hugo, seal of lord abbot Leo, who has accepted this acknowledgment of the homage of the said viscount.

And I, the monk John, have written this charter at the command of the said lord Bernard Atton, viscount of Carcassonne and of his sons, on the day and year given above, in the presence and witness of all those named above.

3. LEGAL RULES FOR HOMAGE AND FEALTY.

Etablissements de St. Louis, II. c. 19. Ed. by Viollet, Vol. II, pp. 395, ff. Old French.

If any one should hold from a lord in fee, he ought to seek his lord within forty days, and if he does not do it within forty days the lord may and ought to seize his fief for default of homage, and the things which should be found there he should seize without return, and yet the vassal would be obliged to pay to his lord the redemption. When any one wishes to enter into the fealty of a lord, he ought to seek him, as we have said above, and should say as follows: "Sir, I request you as my lord, to put me in your fealty and in your homage for such and such a thing situated in your fief, which I have bought." And he ought to say from what man, and this one ought to be present and in the fealty of the lord; and whether it is by purchase or by escheat or by inheritance he ought to explain; and with his hands joined, to speak as follows: "Sir, I become your man and promise to you fealty for the future as my lord towards all men who may live or die, rendering to you such service as the fief requires, making to you your relief as you are the lord." And he ought to say whether for guardianship, or as an escheat, or as an inheritance or as a purchase.

The lord should immediately reply to him: "And I receive you and take you as my man, and give you this kiss as a sign of faith, saving my right and that of others," according to the usage of the various districts.

And the lord may take the revenues and the products of the year, if the relief is not paid to him, and also money rents. But no one makes money payments for a guardianship, or for a dowry, or for a partition, or for a report of the extent of the fief, according to the usages of various districts; except in the one case that the one who holds in guardianship ought to give security to the parties that when the child shall come of age the one who has the guardianship, will do it at his own expense and at his own, and will guarantee the socage tenants for any payments. It is thus in the case of a fief, but in villenage there is no guardianship.

III. SUB-INFEUDATION.

1. FROM THE ENGLISH EXCHEQUER ROLLS, A. D., 1254.

Madox: History of the Exchequer, p. 415. Latin.

Commandment is given to the sheriff of Worcester, that if Baldwin de Frivill does not hold from the king *in capite*, but from Alexander de Abetot, and Alexander from William de Beauchamp, and William from the bishop of Worcester, and the bishop from the king *in capite*, as the same Baldwin says; then the said Baldwin is to have peace from the distraint which has been made upon him for the aid to make the king's son a knight.

2. FROM THE ENGLISH HUNDRED ROLLS, A. D., 1279.

Rotuli Hundredorum, II, 862, 673, and 681 ff. Latin.

Robert de Romeny holds one knight's fee in the vill of Steepleton for homage and his service from William de Leybourne, and he shall pay scutage, when it runs, for one shield, viz: forty shillings; and William de Leybourne holds from the countess of Albemarle, and the countess from the lord king *in capite.*

Roger of St. Germain holds one messuage from Robert of Bedford on the service of paying 3d. to the aforesaid Robert, from whom he holds and of paying 6d. to Richard Hylchester in place of the said Robert, who holds from him. And the said Richard holds from Alan de Chartres, and pays him 2d. a year and Alan from William the Butler, and the same William from lord Gilbert de Neville, and the same Gilbert from the lady Devorguilla de Balliol, and Devorguilla from the king of Scotland, and the same king from the king of England.

Sir Adam de Cretinges holds and accounts in the vill of Stoughton, for four knights' fees from the bishop of Lincoln, and the bishop from the king. The same Adam holds by homage and scutage, when it runs, and has in demesne 13 score acres of arable land and 3 messuages of 2 acres, and 40 acres of woods and 7 acres of meadow and 10 acres of separable pasture.

> 11 villeins, each with a virgate of 20 acres, a house, and some meadow, and each performing certain weekly works, ploughing, etc.
> 16 cottars, each with a cottage and a rood of land, and each paying 12 d. a year and performing certain labor.
> 1 cottar with a half acre, and 2 with houses only.

Sir Anselm de Gyse holds and accounts for two knights' fees, from the same Adam for half a mark a year and for scutage when it happens; and he has in his garden, with a house and vineyard, 6 acres of land; and of arable land 13 score acres, and in meadows 7 acres, and in separable pasture 10 acres and in woods 8 acres.

> 6 villeins, each with 20 acres, etc., as above.

The prior of Bissemede holds one knight's fee from the said Anselm and pays to him scutage when it happens. The same prior has in his garden with the house 8 acres, and 5 score acres of arable land, and 8 acres of woods and 8 acres of meadow, and 6 acres of separable pasture.

> 5 free tenants with a total of 63½ acres of arable land, etc.
> 3 villeins with a total of 1¼ virgates.
> 5 cottars each with a cottage.

Geoffrey, son of Everard of Stoughton holds half a knight's fee from the said Anselm for homage and foreign service, and has in demesne 6 score acres of arable land, and in garden with a messuage one acre and a half and 4 acres of woods and 2 acres of separable pasture.

   1 free holder with 6 acres.

William Schohisfoot holds the twelfth part of one knight's fee from the aforesaid Anselm for homage and foreign service, and has in garden with the house one acre and a half, and in arable land 20 acres, and 3 acres of meadow; and he ought to have common with his beasts in the meadow which is called Mora.

William Dingle holds from the said William one acre and a half of land, and pays annually 1 d.

   Various free and villein tenants holding immediately and mediately from Sir Adam de Cretinges.

IV. MUTUAL DUTIES OF VASSALS AND LORDS.

1. LETTER FROM BISHOP FULBERT OF CHARTRES, A. D., 1020.
   Recueil des Hist. des Gaules et de la France, X, 463. Latin.

To William most glorious duke of the Aquitanians, bishop Fulbert the favor of his prayers.

Asked to write something concerning the form of fealty, I have noted briefly for you on the authority of the books the things which follow. He who swears fealty to his lord ought always to have these six things in memory; what is harmless, safe, honorable, useful, easy, practicable. Harmless, that is to say that he should not be injurious to his lord in his body; safe, that he should not be injurious to him in his secrets or in the defenses through which he is able to be secure; honorable, that he should not be injurious to him in his justice or in other matters that pertain to his honor; useful, that he should not be injurious to him in his possessions; easy or practicable, that that good which his lord is able to do easily, he make not difficult, nor that which is practicable he make impossible to him.

However, that the faithful vassal should avoid these injuries is proper, but not for this does he deserve his holding; for it is not sufficient to abstain from evil, unless what is good is done also. It remains, therefore, that in the same six things mentioned above he should faithfully counsel and aid his lord, if he wishes to be looked upon as worthy of his benefice and to be safe concerning the fealty which he has swor

The lord also ought to act toward his faithful vassal reciprocally in all these things. And if he does not do this he will be justly considered guilty of bad faith, just as the former, if he should be detected in the avoidance of or the doing of or the consenting to them, would be perfidious and perjured.

I would have written to you at greater length, if I had not been occupied with many other things, including the rebuilding of our city and church which was lately entirely consumed in a great fire; from which loss though we could not for a while be diverted, yet by the hope of the comfort of God and of you we breathe again.

2. FROM AN ENGLISH CODE OF THE TWELFTH CENTURY.

Leges Henrici, LXXXII, 3, 4: Thorpe: Anc. Laws and Inst. I, 590. Latin.

And it is allowable to any one, without punishment, to support his lord, if any one assails him, and to obey him in all legitimate ways, except in theft, murder, and in all such things as are not conceded to any one to do and are reckoned infamous by the laws.

The lord ought to do likewise equally with counsel and with aid; and he may come to his man's assistance in his vicissitudes in all ways, without forfeiture.

V. AUTHORITY OF THE LORD OVER THE MARRIAGES OF VASSALS.

1. ACKNOWLEDGMENT OF COUNTESS OF NEVERS, A. D., 1221.

Quantin, Recueil de Pièces du XIII Siècle, No. 274, p. 120. Latin.

I, Matilda, countess of Nevers make known to all who shall see this present letter, that I have sworn upon the sacred gospels to my dearest lord, Philip, by the grace of God, the illustrious king of France, that I will do to him good and faithful service against all living men and women, and that I will not marry except by his will and grace. For keeping these agreements firmly I have given pledges to the same lord king from my men whom I had with me, on their oaths, in this wise, that if I should fail to keep the said agreements with the lord king, (though this shall not be), these are held to come to the lord king with all their lands and fiefs which are held from me, and shall take their oaths to him against me until it shall have been made good to him to his satisfaction. And whenever the lord king shall ask me I will cause him to have similar oaths from my men who were not present with me before the lord king, that is to say from all whom I may have, in good faith, and without evil intention, and similarly the fealty of my town. And in order that this may remain firm and stable, I have written the present letters supported by my seal. Given at Melun, in the year of the Lord 1221, in the month of February.

2. FROM THE CHRONICLE OF LAMBERT OF WATERLOO, A. D. 1151.
Rec. des Hist. des Gaules et de la France, XIII, p. 506. Latin.

Then the young man Aegidius, son of Gerard Maufilatre[1] married a wife, Bertha by name, half-sister of Count Baldwin of Hainault and took her without his assent. The count, extremely angry at this, immediately took up arms against him at the beginning of the month of October. Thus from the time in which he had married her till Whitsunday, with or without consent, he kept her closely by force and arms at his house. But Aegidius having been attacked by a severe fever, which troubled him sharply every day, compelled by the counsel of his friends, who had helped him honorably in all things in his war, dismissed and openly abjured her; and peace was thus restored with the count, and the land was peaceful which had been long troubled by wars.

3. FEES FOR LICENSE TO MARRY, A. D. 1140-1282.
Eng. Exchequer Rolls; Madox: Hist. of Exchequer, pp. 320, 322.

Ralph son of William owes 100 marks as a fine, to be allowed to marry Margery who was wife of Nicholas Corbet who held of the king *in capite*, and that the same Margery may be allowed to marry him.

Walter de Cancy renders account of £15 to be allowed to marry a wife as he shall choose.

Wiverona wife of Iverac of Ipswich renders account of £4 and 1 mark of silver that she may not have to take any husband except the one she wishes.

Emma de Normanville and Roheisa and Margaret and Juliana, her sisters, render account of 10 marks for license to marry where they wish.

---

[1] Hereditary steward of Hainault and a vassal of the count.

Roheisa de Doura renders account of £450 to have half of all the lands which belonged to Richard de Lucy, her grandfather, and which the brother of the same Roheisa had afterward as well in England as in Normandy, and for license to marry where she wishes so long as she does not marry herself to any of the enemies of the king.

Alice, countess of Warwick, renders account of £1000 and 10 palfreys to be allowed to remain a widow as long as she pleases, and not to be forced to marry by the king. And if perchance she should wish to marry, she shall not marry except with the assent and on the grant of the king, where the king shall be satisfied ; and to have the custody of her sons whom she has from the earl of Warwick her late husband.

Hawisa, who was wife of William Fitz Robert renders account of 130 marks and 4 palfreys that she may have peace from Peter of Borough to whom the king has given permission to marry her; and that she may not be compelled to marry.

Geoffrey de Mandeville owes 20,000 marks to have as his wife Isabella, countess of Gloucester, with all the lands and tenements and fiefs which fall to her.

VI. WARDSHIP, RELIEF, AND AIDS.
1. WARDSHIP.
English Exchequer Rolls; Madox : History of the Exchequer, pp. 221, 222.

Thomas de Colville renders an account of 100 marks for having the custody of the sons of Roger Torpel and their land until they come of age.

William, bishop of Ely, owes 220 marks for having the custody of Stephen de Beauchamp with his inheritance and for marrying him where he wishes.

William of St. Mary's church, renders an account of 500 marks for having the custody of the heir of Robert Young, son of Robert Fitzharding, with all his inheritance and all its appurtenances and franchises; that is to say with the services of knights and gifts of churches and marriages of women, and to be allowed to marry him to whatever one of his relatives he wishes; and that all his land is to revert to him freely when he comes of age.

Bartholomew de Muleton renders an account of 100 marks for having the custody of the land and the heiress of Lambert of Ibtoft, and for marrying the wife of the same Lambert to whomsoever he wishes where she shall not be disparaged and that he may be able to confer her (the heiress) upon whom he wishes.

2. RELIEF, FROM THE ENGLISH EXCHEQUER ROLLS, A. D. 1140-1230.
Madox: History of the Exchequer, pp. 216, 218. Latin.

Walter Hait renders an account of 5 marks of silver for the relief of the land of his father.

Walter Brito renders an account of £66, 13s. and 4d. for the relief of his land.

Richard of Estre renders an account of £15 for his relief for 3 knights' fees which he holds from the honor of Mortain.

Walter Fitz Thomas, of Newington, owes 28s. 4d. for having the fourth part of one knights' fee which had been seized into the hand of the king for default of relief.

John of Venetia renders an account of 300 marks for the fine of his land and for the relief of the land which was his father's and he does homage to the king against all mortals.

Ralph, son and heir of Ralph of Sullega renders an account of 100£ for his relief for the lands which were Ralph his father's which he held from the king *in capite*.

John de Balliol owes £150 for the relief of 30 knights' fees which Hugh de Balliol his father held from the king *in capite*, that is 100s. for each fee.

Peter de Bruce renders an account of £100 for his relief for the barony which was of Peter his father.

3. ACKNOWLEDGMENT OF RELIEF, A. D. 1238.
Teulet: Layettes du Trésor des Chartes, No. 2777, Vol. 2, p. 401. Latin.

To all to whom the present writing shall come the nobleman Aimeric, viscount of Châtelherault, greeting. Know that I am held to pay to John de Vineis, bailiff of the lord king, for the *rachat* and relief of the viscounty of Châtelherault 1500 livres of Tours, to be paid to him in the place of the lord king, that is to say, at the coming Ascension 500 livres, and at the feast of All Saints next following 500 livres and at the Purification next following 500 livres. And unless I make complete satisfaction for the said money at the said dates, I agree that he shall seize all my land and all my rents and even my personal property, wherever they may be, until I shall have given complete satisfaction for the above debt.

For the fuller testimony and security of which I have confirmed the present writing with my seal. Given A. D. 1238, in the month of February.

4. THE THREE CUSTOMARY AIDS.

(a) Le Grand Coutumier de Normandie, c. 35 ; Bourdot ; Nouveau Coutumier Général, Vol. IV, p. 18. Old French.

Next it is proper to see the chief aids of Normandy, which are called chief because they should be paid to the chief lords.

In Normandy there are three chief aids. One is to make the oldest son of his lord a knight; the second, to marry his oldest daughter; the third to ransom the body of his lord from prison when he is taken in the Duke's war.

(b) Madox ; History of the Exchequer, pp. 415, 398, 411, notes. Latin.

Aid granted to the king (Henry III.) for the knighting of his eldest son, that is to say from each fee 40s.. The sheriff (of Hereford) renders account of 40s. from John de Balun for one fee, and of £30 from John de Munemul for fifteen fees; the bishop of Hereford renders account of £30 for fifteen fees.

The earl of Clare renders account of £94, 11s. 10d. for the aid for the daughter of the king, for 131 knights and two-thirds of a knight, and a third and a fourth and an eighth and a ninth and a tenth of a knight, and two-thirtieths of a knight of his fee; and for nine knights and the fourth part of a knight of the fee of the countess, his wife.

The abbot of St. Edmund's renders account of 40 marks for the same aid for 40 knights whom he acknowledges he owes to the king.

Of the scutage of knights for the ransom of the lord king. Constance, countess of Brittany, renders account of 140 knights whom Thomas of Borough, steward of the same countess acknowledges before the barons to pertain to the honor of the count of Brittany in England.

VII. MILITARY SERVICE OF TENANTS.

1. AN EARLY FEUDAL SUMMONS, PROBABLY, A. D. 1072.

Quoted in J. H. Round : Feudal England, p. 304. Latin.

W. king of the English to Aethelwig, abbot of Evesham, greeting. I command you to summon all those who are under your charge and jurisdiction to have armed before me by the week after Whitsunday, at Clarendon all the knights which are due to me. And do you also come to me on that day and bring with you armed those five knights which you owe to me from your abbey. Witness Eudo, the steward, at Winchester.

2. GRANT BY AN ABBOT TO A KNIGHT, A. D. 1100.
Historia Monasterii de Abingdon, R. S. Vol. II, p. 135. Latin.

Abbot Faritius also granted to Robert, son of William Mauduit, the land of four hides in Weston which his father had held from the former's predecessor, to be held as a fief. And he should do this service from it, to wit: that whenever the church of Abingdon should perform its knight's service he should do the service of half a knight for the same church; that is to say in castle ward, in military service beyond and on this side the sea, in giving money in proportion to the knights on the capture of the king, and in the rest of the services which the other knights of the church perform. He also does homage to the same abbot. This land previously did the service of three weeks yearly only.

3. MILITARY HOLDINGS IN ENGLAND, A. D. 1279.
Rotuli Hundredorum: Vol. II, pp. 711, 710. Latin.

The jurors say that Robert Fitz Nigel holds the manor of Iftele in chief from the king for doing the service of one knight's fee in the service of the lord king when he is in the army, at his own cost, and afterward, if he shall be required, at the cost of the lord king.

The manor of Hedington with its hamlets and all its appurtenances is of the ancient demesne of the crown of the lord king and is held in chief from the lord king for £20, at the two terms of the year, to be paid to the Exchequer of the lord king, that is to say, at Easter £10 and at Michaelmas £10. And Hugh de Plesens is feudatory of the lord king, since he is responsible to him for one knight's fee when scutage runs, or he must go with the lord king when he is in the army and serve him for forty days at his own cost, for the aforesaid manor, and if he makes a longer stay, at the expense of the lord king. . . . . . . Hugh de Plesens holds the manor of Hedington.

4. ACKNOWLEDGMENT OF MILITARY DUTY, A. D. 1212.
Quantin: Rec. de Pièces du XIII Siècle, No. 116, p. 53. Latin.

William, by the grace of God bishop of Auxerre to all who shall see these presents, greeting in the Lord. Know that we acknowledge that we owe to our lord Philip, illustrious king of the French, military service, as is the common service of bishops and barons; and this for the future we will perform through our knights, as others. For the same lord king has released our person from the service of the army so long as we live.

5. ETABLISSEMENTS DE ST. LOUIS, A. D 1270.
Livre I, ch. 65; Ed. by Viollet, Vol. II, p. 95. Old French.

The baron and all vassals of the king are bound to appear before him when he shall summon them, and to serve him at their own expense for forty days and forty nights, with as many knights as each one owes; and he is able to exact from them these services when he wishes and when he has need of them. And if the king wishes to keep them more than forty days at their own expense, they are not bound to remain if they do not wish it. And if the king wishes to keep them at his expense for the defence of the realm, they are bound to remain. And if the king wishes to lead them outside of the kingdom, they need not go unless they wish to, for they have already served their forty days and forty nights.

6. SERVICE OF THE COUNT OF CHAMPAGNE.
Matthew Paris: Chronica Majora, R. S.; III, 116. Latin.

Then Louis, king of the French in order to escape from the pestilence, which was raging with great severity in the camp (before Avignon), betook himself to a certain abbey called Montpensier, which was not far distant from the siege works, till the city should be captured. There came to him at that place Henry, count of Champagne, who had passed forty days at the siege, asking license to return to his own possessions, according to the custom of France. When the king refused his permission the count replied that when his military service of forty days had been performed, he was not bound nor was he willing to remain longer. The king, however, was so inflamed by anger at this that he declared with an oath that if the count should withdraw then he would devastate his whole land with fire. Then the count, as the story goes, procured poison to be placed in the drink of the king, on account of his desire for the queen, for whom he had a guilty love, and was so impelled by the incentive of lust that he was not able to brook longer delay. When the count had thus gone away the king grew desperately sick, and the poison reaching his vital parts, he came to his end; although others say that it was not from poison but from dysentery that he died.

7. **FRENCH MILITARY TENANTS SUMMONED TO THE ROYAL ARMY.**
Rec. des Hist. des Gaules et de la France, XXIII, pp. 753 ff. Latin.

In the year 1272 the bishop of Paris came to Tours at the citation of the lord king and presented himself in the king's house on the second Sunday after Easter, before Ferrario de Verneuil, knight, marshall of France, saying that he had come at the citation of the lord king prepared to fulfill his duty; who replied to him that he should come again or send at the first hour of the next day, because in the meanwhile he could not speak or respond to him, since Gregory of St. Martin of Tours was absent, on account of his weakness, and because, moreover, he was expecting new instructions from the king. On the next day and on Tuesday the aforesaid bishop presented himself before the said marshall, saying that he had come ready for the service of the king with three knights, whose names were John de Marchiaco, John de Juliaco and Adam de Blesum. He said that if he was held to send more he was ready to do what he ought; and if he had furnished more than he owed, that this should not bind either him or the church of Paris for the future.

The bishop of Troyes appeared for his see, saying that he owed two knights, whose names were Ralph and Droco de Pratellis.

John de Rouvraye, knight, lord of Yneto, appeared for himself acknowledging that he owed one knight by reason of his land of Rouvraye, whom he brought with him, that is to say, John de Caim.

Reginald Trihan, knight, appeared for himself and goes.[1]

Henry d'Eauville did not appear, but he sent for himself one knight, William de Petra.

William Bacon, knight, appeared for Geoffrey de Forêt, who owes military service for forty days; he goes to the army.

William de Coynères, knight, sends for himself Thomas Chocquet, for ten days.

Thomas de Cugry, esquire, appeared, saying that he owes four days; he sends instead of himself Richard de St. Germain, who will complete these four days after his own service.

Nicholas Bourdet, esquire, appeared for himself, and goes to the army; and he will be a knight there, or will provide another knight.

John de Chanteleu, knight, appeared saying that he owed ten days for himself, and that he also appeared for Godardus de Godardville, knight, who owes forty days.

Robert de Morville, knight, appeared for himself, owing military service for twenty days for half a fee.

The count of Soissons appeared and went to the army with three other knights whom he acknowledges he owes to the king, and led with him six knights besides his service.

Hugh de Conflans, knight, marshal of Champagne, appeared for the king of Navarre and led with him sixty knights for service owed to the king.

John Doré, knight, appeared for the lady of Chapelle, on account of her land of Berry which owes military service; and he goes in place of her.

William de Chantelon, knight, appeared for himself saying that he owed military service to the lord king for thirty days, for three-quarters of a knight's fee.

VIII. FEUDAL JUSTICE.

1. ENGLISH CUSTOMS OF ELEVENTH CENTURY.

Leges Henrici Primi, LV. Thorpe: Anc. Laws and Inst., Vol. I. p. 55.   Latin.

To every lord it is allowed to summon his man that he may be at right to him in his court; and even if he is resident at the most distant manor of that honor from which he holds, he shall go to the plea if his lord summons him. If his lord holds different fiefs the man of one honor is not compelled by law to go to another plea, unless the cause belongs to the other to which his lord has summoned him.

If a man holds from several lords and honors, however much he holds from others, he owes most and will be subject for justice to him of whom he is the liege man.

Every vassal owes to his lord fidelity concerning his life and members and earthly honor and keeping of his counsel in what is honorable and useful saving the faith of God and of the prince of the land. Theft, however, and treason and murder and whatever things are against the Lord and the catholic faith are to be required of or performed by no one; but faith shall be held to all lords, saving the faith of the earlier, and the more to the one of which he is the liege. And let permission be given him, if any of his men seek another lord for himself.

2. WRIT TO SECURE FEUDAL JURISDICTION, AB. A. D. 1100.
Chronicon Monasterii de Abingdon, Vol. II, p. 165, Rolls Series. Latin.

Henry, king of England, to Ralph Basset, greeting.

I command you to cause Vincent, abbot of Abingdon to have his court in Oxford as well and fully as that church of Abingdon ever had it or any one of his predecessors had it best and most fully and honorably. And his men shall not plead outside of his court unless the abbot has first failed to give right in his court, and as you are able to make inquisition through the legal men of Oxford that he ought to have his court. Witness the chancellor; at Woodstock.

3. ETABLISSEMENTS DE ST. LOUIS.
Livre I. c. 71 : Ed. by Viollet, Vol. II, p. 124. French.

If a baron is summoned to the court of the king for any question of an inheritance and shall say, "I am not willing to be judged in this matter except by my peers," then at least three others ought to be summoned, and the king's justice shall try the suit along with these and any other nobles.

4. CONDEMNATION BY A FEUDAL COURT.
Teulet : Layettes du Trésor des Chartes, No. 3778, Vol. 3, p. 70. Latin.

Raymond by the grace of God count of Toulouse, marquis of Provence, to the nobleman Arnold Atton, viscount of Lomagne, greeting.

Let it be known to your nobility, by the tenor of these presents what has been done in the matter of the complaints which we have made about you before the court of Agen; that you have not taken the trouble to keep or fulfil the agreements sworn by you to us, as is more fully contained in the instrument drawn up there, sealed with our seal by the public notary; and that you have refused contemptuously to appear before the said court for the purpose of doing justice; and otherwise committed multiplied and great delinquencies against us. As your faults have required, the aforesaid court of Agen has unanimously and concordantly pronounced sentence against you, and for these matters has condemned you to hand over and restore to us the chateau of Auvillars and all that land which you hold from us in fee, to be had and held by us by right of the obligation by which you have bound it to us for fulfilling and keeping the said agreements.

Likewise it has declared that we are to be put into possession of the said land and that it is to be handed over to us, on account of your contumacy, because you have not been willing to appear before the same court on the days which were assigned to you. Moreover, it has declared that you shall be held and required to restore the said land in whatsoever way we wish to receive it, with few or many, in peace or in anger, in our own person, by right of lordship. Likewise it has declared that you shall restore to us all the expenses which we have incurred or the court itself has incurred on those days which were assigned to you or because of those days, and has condemned you to repay these to us.

Moreover, it has declared that the nobleman Gerald d'Armagnac, whom you hold captive, you shall liberate, and deliver him free to us. We will, moreover, by right of our lordship that you liberate him.

We call, therefore, upon your discretion in this matter, strictly requiring you and commanding that you obey the aforesaid sentences in all things and fulfil them in all respects and in no way defer the fulfilment of them. For making the announcement, the demand and the reception of these things, we have appointed as our representatives our beloved and faithful noblemen Gaston de Gontaud and R. Bernard de Balencs, promising that whatever shall be done by them in the aforesaid matters, we will hold as settled and firm forever. In testimony of which we have caused these present letters to be corroborated by the strength of our seal. Similar letters, divided through the alphabet, for a perpetual memory of this matter we have caused to be retained with us. Given at Agen, the third of the Kalends of July, A. D. 1249.

IX. RIGHT OF COINAGE.

1. GRANT OF THE MINT OF AUXERRE, A. D. 1204.

Quantin : Recueil de Pièces du XIII Siècle, No. 35, p. 17. Latin.

I, Pierre, count of Auxerre and Tonnerre, make known to all present and to come that since Lambert de Bar possessed by hereditary right the dies of the mint of Auxerre and Tonnerre, and on that account was my man; on his petition I have granted the said dies to my beloved and faithful Pierre de Chablis and his heirs to be possessed peacefully and quietly forever. And on this account with the consent and good will of the countess Yolande, my wife, I have received the aforesaid Pierre as my liege man. For the confirmation of this matter I and Yolande, the countess, my wife, have given command that the present charter corroborated with the protection of our seals should be delivered to the said Pierre.

Done in the year of the Incarnation of the Lord 1204, in the month of July.

2. CHARTER OF ODO OF BURGUNDY, A. D. 1337.
Ducange, under the word Moneta regia. Latin.

We, Odo, duke of Burgundy, count of Artois and Burgundy, palatine and lord of Sains make known to all that since we have heard that our dear and famous lord, the king of France, feels hardly toward us because his master of the mint has given him to understand that we are now coining money in our town of Auxerre like his money in imprint and form, that there is little difference between his money and ours, and that many people may be deceived in taking our money as the money of our said lord; we who would not on any account wish to do anything which should be displeasing to our lord, are willing and do promise to change the imprint in the form which we are now having coined in our town of Auxerre, and to make in our said money such a difference and such a form that each person will be able clearly to distinguish our money from the money of the lord king, so that our said money will have its circulation only in our county of Burgundy and in the land of the Empire. Moreover we will command and forbid and cause to be forbidden that money of the kingdom should be minted, and also cause oath to be made that the small coin of the kingdom shall not be received.

In testimony of which thing we have caused our seal to be placed upon these present letters, made and given at the Bois de Vincennes the third day of October, 1337.

X. FORFEITURE.

Rotuli Hundredorum, ii, p. 183. Latin.

It is presented by the jurors above named that the manor of Chinnore along with the hamlet of Sydenham was held of old, from the time of the Conquest, from the lord king of England, by a certain man who was named Walter de Vernon, as one knight's fee; and because the said Walter de Vernon refused to perform his due service from the said manor to the lord king John in the time of the war which sprang up between the lord king John and the king of France, the lord king John with the advice of his council seized that same manor with its appurtenances and removed the said Walter de Vernon, on account of his ingratitude from the possession of the aforesaid manor forever. And the lord king John granted that same manor with its appurtenances for the services that to the same lord king was due from it to Saer de Quincy formerly earl of Winchester, to hold to himself and his heirs *in capite* from the lord king as one knight's fee; and the heirs of the said Saer held the aforesaid manor in succession, and still hold it, except the hamlet of Sydenham, which the abbot of Thame holds as a gift from Roger de Quincy.

BIBLIOGRAPHICAL NOTE.

Ch. Mortet : Féodalité.

Perhaps the best general treatise on the subject is the article by this author given under the word *Féodalité*, in *La Grande Encyclopédie*, and subsequently reprinted as a separate work.

A. Luchaire: Manuel des Institutions Françaises, Pt. II. Les Institutions Féodales.

This is a detailed description of feudal institutions from the 11th to the 14th century and abounds in bibliographical information. It does not deal with the question of the origins of Feudalism. Upon this last question there has been a very considerable amount of writing, largely polemical in its character. Some of the most conspicuous books on this phase of the subject are the following:

P. Roth: Geschichte des Beneficialwesens, 1850; *and* Feudalität und Unterthanenverband, 1863.

G. Waitz: Ueber die Anfänge der Vassalität, 1856; *and* Deutsche Verfassungsgeschichte, Vol. IV, 1884.

Fustel de Coulanges: Les Origines du Système Féodal, 1890.

Very useful and suggestive outline accounts of Feudalism are to be found in English in Professor E. Emerton's *Introduction to the Middle Ages*, and *Mediæval Europe;* and Professor G. B. Adams' *Civilization during the Ages.*

SERIES FOR 1894.

I. Early Reformation Period in England.* Single number, 20 pages.
II. Urban and the Crusaders.* Single number, 24 pages.
III. The Reaction after 1815.* Single number, 24 pages.
IV. Letters of the Crusaders.* Double number, 40 pages.
V. The French Revolution, 1789-1791.* Double number, 36 pages.
VI. English Constitutional Documents.* Double number, 36 pages.

SERIES FOR 1895.

I. English Towns and Gilds. Double number, 40 pages.
II. Napoleon and Europe. Double number, 32 pages.
III. The Mediæval Student. Single number, 20 pages.
IV. Monastic Tales of the XIII Century. Single number, 20 pages.
V. England in the Time of Wycliffe. Single number, 20 pages.
VI. Period of Early Reformation in Germany. Double number, 32 pages.
VII. Life of St. Columban. Double number, 36 pages.

SERIES FOR 1896.

I. The Fourth Crusade. Single number, 20 pages.
II. Statistical Documents of the Middle Ages. Single number, 23 pages.
III. Period of the Later Reformation. Double number, 32 pages.
IV. The Witch-Persecutions. Double number, 36 pages.
V. English Manorial Documents. Double number, 32 pages.
VI. The Pre-Reformation Period. Double number, 34 pages.

SERIES FOR 1897.

I. The Early Christian Persecutions. Double number, 32 pages.
II. Canons and Creeds of the First Four Councils. Double number, Apr.
III. Documents Illustrative of Feudalism. Double number, 36 pages.
IV. Ordeals, Compurgation, Excommunication, and Interdict. Double number, 34 pages.
V. Typical Cahiers of 1789. Double number, 36 pages.

SERIES FOR 1898.

I. Monumentum Ancyranum. (About 80 pages.) Ready in May.
II. Remonstrance of the *Cour des Aides*, May, 1775. (About 100 pages.) Ready in November.

Annual subscription, $1.00.
Single numbers, Vol. I, 15 cents; Vols. II, III and IV, 10 cents.
Double numbers, Vol. I, 25 cents; Vols. II, III and IV, 20 cents.
Numbers in Vol. V, unbound, 60 cents; bound, 80 cents, each.
Bound Volumes, $1.50.
Discounts will be given on orders for 25 or more numbers.
Subscriptions and orders should be sent to

DANA C. MUNRO,

UNIVERSITY OF PENNSYLVANIA,

April, 1898. Philadelphia, Pa.

---

* Revised edition.

Vol. IV.  No. 4.

Translations and Reprints

FROM THE

Original Sources of European History

ORDEALS, COMPURGATION, EXCOMMUNICATION,
AND INTERDICT.

EDITED BY ARTHUR C. HOWLAND, PH.D.
University of Illinois.

PUBLISHED BY

The Department of History of the University of Pennsylvania.

Philadelphia, Pa., 1898.
ENGLISH AGENCY: P. S. KING & SON, 12-14 King Street, London, S. W.

Price, 20 Cents.

THE use by readers and students of those original documents from which our knowledge of history is so largely drawn has come to be valued in recent times at something like its true worth. The sequence of past events, the form and spirit of institutions, the characters of men, the prevailing habits of thought, obtain their greatest reality when we study them in the very words used by the men to whom the past was the living present. Even historians who have not been characterized by a close dependence on the results of patient investigation of the sources have recognized the superiority of an appeal to original testimony. Mr. Froude says, "Whenever possible, let us not be told about this man or that. Let us hear the man himself speak, let us see him act, and let us be left to form our own opinion about him." And in "Stones of Venice," Mr. Ruskin writes, "the only history worth reading is that written at the time of which it treats, the history of what was done and seen, heard out of the mouths of the men who did and saw. One fresh draught of such history is worth more than a thousand volumes of abstracts, and reasonings, and suppositions and theories."

Experience has proved, not only that the interest of students can be more readily obtained through the vividness of a direct and first-hand presentation, and that knowledge thus gained is more tangible and exact; but that the critical judgment is developed in no slight degree, and the ability as well as the interest for further study thus secured.

The utilization of the original sources of history has, however, been much restricted by their comparative inaccessibility. A great proportion of such documents as illustrate European history exist only in more or less unfamiliar languages; many are to be found only in large and expensive collections, or in works that are out of print and therefore difficult to obtain or consult.

. . The desire to overcome in some degree this inaccessibility, especially for their own classes, led the editors of the present series of translations and reprints from the original sources of European history to undertake its publication. During the past three years evidence has been given of the usefulness of the documents in several directions. Their most considerable use has naturally been with college classes. One or more of the issues has been used in twenty-four of the principal Universities and Colleges, and four Divinity Schools. In addition to these and their use in lower schools they have been found to give increased value to University Extension courses and reading circles.

During the current year the series will consist of five "double numbers" of 32 pages or more, each. The separate numbers will be edited respectively by Dana Carleton Munro, A.M. and Edith Bramhall, A.M., of the University of Pennsylvania, Edwin Knox Mitchell, of Hartford Theological Seminary, Edward P. Cheyney, A.M., of the University of Pennsylvania, Arthur C. Howland, Ph. D., of the University of Illinois, and Merrick Whitcomb, Ph.D., of the University of Pennsylvania. Titles of the numbers and further particulars are given on the third cover page.

TRANSLATIONS AND REPRINTS
FROM THE
ORIGINAL SOURCES OF EUROPEAN HISTORY.

VOL. IV.	TYPICAL CAHIERS OF 1789.	No. 5

TABLE OF CONTENTS.

		PAGE
I.	CAHIER OF CLERGY, BAILLIAGE OF BLOIS, ...	2
II.	CAHIER OF NOBILITY, BAILLIAGE OF BLOIS, ...	8
III.	CAHIER OF THIRD ESTATE, BAILLIAGE OF VERSAILLES, . .	24

INTRODUCTORY NOTE.

It has been the effort of the editor to present, as nearly as possible, a complete cahier of each of the three orders. It is in the study of a single cahier that the trend of pre-revolutionary thought and aspiration may best be recognized. From this as a starting-point the student may proceed to acquaint himself with the variations of criticism and suggestion afforded by a comparison of many cahiers. Something of this kind has already been done by Mr. E. J. Lowell, in his *Eve of the French Revolution*, chapters XXI and XXII.

In selecting typical cahiers for presentation, an effort has been made to avoid the cahiers of localities whose conditions were exceptional. Such cahiers are for the most part filled with grievances and demands of a purely local nature. For this and other reasons two cahiers of Blois have been selected. The cahier of the Third Estate of Blois, however, was rejected. This document has shared a fate common to many of the cahiers of the Third Estate. The local cahiers of the smaller political divisions of the bailliage of Blois have fallen into the hands of lawyers, who have assembled and combined them with an eye single to their own desires and interests, reducing all other considerations to the simplest terms. The cahier of Versailles seems to have been somewhat more fortunate.

The cahiers of the Nobility are the most interesting. They are original compositions, drawn up by men of the highest intelligence and patriotism, men not devoid of sympathy with the intellectual movements of their time, and thoroughly alive to the necessity of reorganization. The clergy were less susceptible to the influences of the time, and their cahiers are more self-conscious. The method of assembling the local cahiers of the Third Estate resulted in a loss of vigor and personality. The ingenuousness and local coloring, which give the original cahiers an exceptional interest, are lost in the necessary process of condensation.

In the following text a French word here and there has been retained, mainly for the reason that no brief English equivalent has suggested itself. These terms may be found explained for the most part in Mr. Lowell's book, cited above; and for a wider discussion the student may consult Chéruel : *Dictionnaire historique des institutions, moeurs et coutumes de la France*, or to better purpose, *La Grande Encyclopédie*.

I. CAHIER,

Containing the grievances of the order of the clergy of the bailliage of Blois and of the secondary bailliage of Romorantin.

Archives Parlementaires, Vol. II, pp. 373-378.

FIRST DIVISION.
Religion.

[This division, which relates almost exclusively to the affairs of the French church, has been omitted as being of relatively small importance to the general student. It is worthy of note, however, that Art. 1-3 deplore the extension of religious liberty to non-catholics and the growing freedom of the press.]

SECOND DIVISION.
Constitution.

The clergy of the *bailliage* of Blois have never believed that the constitution needed reform. Nothing is wanting to assure the welfare of king and people except that the present constitution should be religiously and inviolably observed.

The constitutional principles concerning which no doubt can be entertained are:

1. That France is a true monarchy, where a single man rules and is ruled by law alone.

2. That the general laws of the kingdom may be enacted only with the consent of the king and the nation. If the king proposes a law, the nation accepts or rejects it; if the nation demands a law, it is for the king to consent or to reject it; but in either case it is the king alone who upholds the law in his name and attends to its execution.

3. That in France we recognize as king him to whom the crown belongs by hereditary right according to the Salic law.

4. That we recognize the nation in the States General, composed of the three orders of the kingdom, which are the clergy, the nobility and the third estate.

5. That to the king belongs the right of assembling the States General, whenever he considers it necessary.

For the welfare of the kingdom we ask, in common with the whole nation, that this convocation be periodical and fixed, as we particularly desire, at every five years, except in the case of the next meeting, when the great number of matters to be dealt with makes a less remote period desirable.

6. That the States General should not vote otherwise than by order.

7. That the three orders are equal in power and independent of each other, in such a manner that their unanimous consent is necessary to the expression of the nation's will.

8. That no tax may be laid without the consent of the nation.

9. That every citizen has, under the law, a sacred and inviolable right to personal liberty and the possession of his goods.

We regard *lettres de cachet* as an abuse, contrary to the constitution. Each citizen without distinction ought to be subject to the laws and other rules of justice, and his trial by any special commission whatsoever not permitted.

The expense which the convocation of the States General will entail, through the necessary disturbance of citizens in their residence and vocations, ought to be diminished by a simplification of the forms of procedure.

A consideration of the proportion which ought to be established between the representatives of the higher and the lower clergy moves us to ask of the King that for the future the two divisions of the order shall hold their elections separately, and that in the lower division of the clerical order the forms of election shall be such that no member of the bodies which compose the order may be deprived of the representation which is his due.

The provincial estates or assemblies seem to us to constitute the régime likely to produce the best results in all branches of administration. We beseech the King to give them a legal existence and to organize them with a view to preserving the requisite balance between the interests involved, according to the clergy a number of representatives equal to that of the nobility.

THIRD DIVISION.

Taxes.

declare that for the future they desire to sustain the burden of taxation in common with other subjects of the king. They believe that it will be necessary for the States General, in order to bring within reasonable limits the burden of taxation, which has become excessive, to ascertain accurately the state of finances, together with the amounts of income and expenditure, and that an effort should be made to restrict the expenses of the court and of all departments, in so far as the needs of the state and the splendor of the nation will permit, and to fix the interest upon the state debt at a moderate rate, which is just, since the nation itself guarantees the payment.

To render all ministers and other persons charged with the management of finances responsible with their persons and property for their administration; to confide this administration, in so far as possible, to councils, bureaux and associations, rather than to private individuals who are more easily deceived and seduced; to fix the bases for general and special assessment; to simplify the collection of taxes, and to fix upon wise and patriotic means, which, while assuring the payment into the royal treasury of the last penny due, shall insure protection for the people against those persecutions which are ruinous to the public welfare.

The reforms which we judge most necessary in the matter of taxes, and which we particularly recommend to His Majesty's attention are the following:

1. In the *gabelles* and *aides*, which ought to be suppressed, or replaced, if need be, with a tax less burdensome;

2. In export duties, which we desire to see restricted to the frontier;

3. In registry fees, which have grown to an exorbitant figure. The irregularity of these charges subjects citizens to frequent contentions;

4. It is desirable to lessen the disadvantage under which poor country people labor in securing justice in the matter of over-taxation and malversations, on account of the considerable advances which they have to make in order to bring the matter to an issue;

5. The shifting of certain taxes might bring them to bear upon various articles of luxury and especially upon unnecessary articles of domestic use.

The best interests of the kingdom, which His Majesty will never cease to regard, seem to us to demand the following:

1. That no tax shall be laid without the consent of the nation;

2 That the King shall resume possession of all portions of the do-

main which have been illegally alienated, and even of those portions whose alienation, although accompanied with the forms of law, has nevertheless worked a manifest injury to the royal interests;

3. That the domain shall be declared inalienable for the future;

4. That the collectors of the *centième dernier*, due upon collateral successions, donations, etc., shall be obliged to give notice *gratis* for at least a month before the expiration of the term of payment;

5. That *franc-fiefs* shall be suppressed as useless and burdensome;

6. That the taxes approved by the States General shall be laid for a limited time only, subject to whatever arrangement may be made for the convocation of future States General.

FOURTH DIVISION.
Justice.

For the purpose of securing a reform of the principal abuses in the administration of justice we very humbly present to His Majesty what appears to us of first importance:

1. To divide the too extensive jurisdiction of the sovereign courts;

2. To complete the number of judges in each *bailliage*, in order that sessions may be held with greater regularity;

3. To suppress all judges of exceptional courts;

4. To suppress all seignorial courts in cases where a justice and necessary officials have not been retained and salaried by the *seigneurs*;

5. To authorize vassals to refuse the jurisdiction of their *seigneurs* in suits against the said *seigneurs*;

6. To establish in the principal rural places justices of the peace for the trial of minor cases;

7. To prevent excessive and illegal charges before judges and magistrates;

8. To ordain that these charges shall not be imposed except with the consent of that portion of the nation over which these judges and magistrates are to be placed;

9. To simplify the forms of justice by reducing costs, by accelerating procedure and by suppressing judges' fees;

10. To reform the civil and criminal codes and to diminish the number of customary codes which prevail in various parts of the kingdom, in order to hasten the day, if possible, when there shall be but one national code;

To ordain that authorization shall not be given by the bureau of mortgages until two months after the notice of foreclosure, which notice shall be given at the close of the parish mass, as well at the place where the property is situated, as at the residence of the vendor, and that the bailiff be compelled to obtain the signatures of two residents of each parish upon his proof of service;

11. To abolish the offices of appraiser, vendor of chattels, receivers of consignment etc., as involving useless costs.

FIFTH DIVISION.
Nobility, the chase, etc.

The nobility ought to be assured of their prerogatives and distinctions in the state, and we very humbly beseech His Majesty to grant these only as a reward for services rendered to our native land.

The King is moreover entreated to take into consideration:

1. The great number of serious abuses which the right of the chase entails upon agriculturists, and the annoyances caused them by game-keepers;

2. The evils which result from the right of open warren;

3. The importance of the regulations concerning pigeon-houses, which have almost ceased to be observed;

4. The injustice of depriving the inhabitants of lands adjacent to forests, as has been done in many localities, of the right of pasture, and other rights, which have been accorded them on various accounts.

SIXTH DIVISION.
Commerce.

We beseech His Majesty:

1. To take the most effectual means of preventing bankruptcies;

2. To fix a term, after which prisoners for debt may recover their liberty;

3. To interest himself in ameliorating the condition of negroes in the colonies.

Impressed as we are with the great influence of public education upon the religion, morals and prosperity of the state, we beseech His Majesty to favor it with all his power. We desire:

1. That public instruction shall be absolutely gratuitous, as well in the universities as in the provincial schools;

2. That the provincial *collèges* shall be entrusted by preference to the corporations of the regular clergy;

3. That many corporations of the regular clergy, which at present are not occupied with the instruction of youth, shall apply themselves to this work, and thereby render themselves more useful to the state;

4. That in towns too small to support a *collège* there shall be at least one or more masters, according to the importance of the place, who shall be able to teach the principles of Latinity or the humanities, and that their salaries shall be sufficient to allow of absolutely gratuitous instruction;

5. That this instruction shall be under the supervision of the parish priests and municipal officers;

6. That each candidate seeking permission to teach shall be obliged to produce proofs of correct life and habits, and give evidence of his capacity in an examination before the principal and professors of the nearest *collège*.

7. That masters of schools shall not employ as assistants persons from other localities, unless such persons shall have pursued the same vocation for at least two years in the place where they have studied, and shall be furnished with references and recognized as competent by means of an examination, as above indicated;

That, for the purpose of facilitating the education of girls, communities of religious women, whatever may be their institution, shall be obliged to open free public schools for girls under the supervision of the parish priests.

We beseech His Majesty that after the examination, which shall be made in the States General of the *cahiers* of the various *bailliages* of the kingdom, this work shall be made public by means of the press, both for the satisfaction of constituents and for the honor of the deputies.

(*This document, recorded in the clerk's office of the bailliage of Blois is signed: Abbé Ponthèves, President.*" *Then follow the signatures of 53 parish priests, 14 priors, 8 canons, 8 priests, 3 deans, 3 abbots, 3 curates, one chaplain, one friar, one deacon and 27 persons unclassified.*)

II. INSTRUCTIONS,

Given by the nobility of the bailliage of Blois to the viscount of Beauharnois and the cavalier de Phélines, deputies of the order to the States General, and to M. Lavoisier, supplementary deputy, March 28, 1789.

Archives Parlementaires, Vol. II, pp. 378-385.

The object of every social institution is to confer the greatest possible happiness upon those who live under its laws.

Happiness ought not to be confined to a small number of men; it belongs to all. It is not an exclusive privilige to be contested for; it is a common right which must be preserved, which must be shared, and the public happiness is a source from which each has a right to draw his supply.

Such are the sentiments which animate the nobility of the *bailliage* of Blois, at a moment when we are called upon by the sovereign to give our representatives to the nation. These principles have occupied all our thoughts during the preparation of this *cahier*: May they animate all citizens of this great state! May they evoke that spirit of union, that unanimity of desires which shall erect upon an indestructible foundation of power the prosperity of the nation, the welfare of the monarch and his subjects!

Deep and established ills cannot be cured with a single effort: the destruction of abuses is not the work of a day. Alas! of what avail to reform them if their causes be not removed? The misfortune of France arises from the fact that it has never had a fixed constitution. A virtuous and sympathetic king seeks the counsels and coöperation of the nation to establish one: let us hasten to accomplish his desires; let us hasten to restore to his soul that peace which his virtues merit. The principles of this constitution should be simple; they may be reduced to two: *Security for person, security for property;* because, in fact, it is from these two fertile principles that all organization of the body politic takes its rise.

PERSONAL LIBERTY.

Art. 1. In order to assure the exercise of this first and most sacred of the rights of man, we ask that no citizen may be exiled, arrested or held prisoner except in cases contemplated by the law and in accord-

That in case the States General determine that provisional detention may be necessary at times, it ought to be ordained that every person so arrested shall be delivered, within twenty-four hours, into the hands of appropriate judges, to be judged with the least possible delay, in conformity with the laws of the kingdom; that evocations be abolished, and that no extraordinary commission be established in any instance; finally that no person be deprived of his position, civil or military, without judgment in due form.

Since individual liberty is a right equally sacred for citizens of all ranks and classes, without distinction or precedence, the States General are invited to interest themselves in the suppression of all forced service in the militia and of acts of authority which involve the violation of personal rights, and which are the more intolerable in a century of intelligence, when it is possible to accomplish the same end with less oppressive means. The application of these principles ought to suffer exception only in the case of an urgent necessity, when the safety of the country is at stake, in which case the extent of the executive power should be enlarged.

From the right of personal liberty arises the right to write, to think, to print and to publish, with the names of authors and publishers, all kinds of complaints and reflections upon public and private affairs, limited by the right of every citizen to seek in the established courts legal redress against author or publisher, in case of defamation or injury; limited also by all restrictions which the States General may see fit to impose in that which concerns morals and religion.

The violation of the secrecy of letters is still an infringement upon the liberty of citizens; and since the sovereign has assumed the exclusive right of transporting letters throughout the kingdom, and this has become a source of public revenue, such carriage ought to be made under the seal of confidence.

We indicate further a number of instances in which natural liberty is abridged:

1. The abuse of police regulations, which every year, in an arbitrary manner and without regular process, thrusts a number of artisans and useful citizens into prisons, work-houses and places of detention, often for trivial faults and even upon simple suspicion;

2. The abuse of exclusive privileges which fetter industry;

3. The gilds and corporations which deprive citizens of the righ of using their faculties;

4. The regulations governing manufactures, the rights of inspection and *marque*, which impose restrictions that have lost their usefulness, and which burden industry with a tax that yields no profit to the public treasury.

TAXES.

Art. 2. A tax is a partition of property.

This partition ought not to be otherwise than voluntary; in any other case the rights of property are violated: Hence it is the indefeasable and inalienable right of the nation to consent to its taxes.

According to this principle, which has been solemnly recognized by the king, no tax, real or personal, direct or indirect, nor any contribution whatsoever, under whatsoever name or form, may be established except with the consent and free and voluntary approval of the nation. Nor may said power of consenting to a tax be transferred or delegated by the nation to any magistracy or other body, or exercised by the provincial estates nor by the provincial, city or communal assemblies: superior and inferior courts shall be especially charged to attend to the execution of this article, and to prosecute as exactors those who may undertake to levy a tax which has not received the proper sanction.

All public loans are, properly speaking, taxes in disguise, since the property of the kingdom is affected and hypothecated for the payment of capital and interest. Therefore no loan, under whatsoever form or denomination, may be effected without the consent and will of the nation assembled.

Since the greater number of the taxes and imposts established up to this time have not received the sanction of the nation, the first business of the assembled estates will be to abolish all without exception; at the same time, in order to avoid the inconvenience resulting from an interruption in the payment of interest on the public debt and the expenses of government, the nation assembled, by virtue of the same authority, shall re-establish them, collecting them under the title of a free gift during the session of the States General and up to the time when they shall have established such other taxes as may seem to them desirable.

A tax is no other thing than a voluntary sacrifice which each person makes of his particular property in favor of the public power which protects and guarantees all. It is therefore evident that the tax ought to be proportioned to the interest which each has in preserving his property, and consequently to the value of this property. In accordance with this principle the nobility of the *bailliage* of Blois believes itself in duty bound to lay at the feet of the nation all the pecuniary exemptions which it has enjoyed or might have enjoyed up to this time, and it offers to contribute to the public needs in proportion with other citizens, upon condition that the names of *taille* and *corvée* be suppressed and all direct taxes be comprised in a single land tax in money.

The nobility of the *bailliage* of Blois, in making this surrender of its ancient privileges, has been unable to suppress a sentiment of interest in favor of that portion of the nobility which a modest fortune confines to the rural districts. It believes that a proprietor, who fulfils the obligation of his heritage, spreads about him prosperity and happiness; that the efforts he makes to increase his revenues increase at the same time the mass of the agricultural products of the realm; that the country districts are covered with chateaux and manors, formerly inhabited by the French nobility, but to-day abandoned; that a great public interest would be subserved by inducing proprietors to seek again, so far as possible, their interests in the country.

Animated by these motives we believe that it is our duty to solicit the especial protection of the States General in favor of that respectable portion of the nation, which divides its time between the culture of the fields and the defence of the state; and we hope that means will be found to reconcile that which is due to their interests and needs with the absolute renunciation which is about to be made of the pecuniary exemptions of nobility.

If, as has been said, a tax is the price paid for the protection which government accords to property, it follows that all property which the government protects ought to be subject to the tax; that the tax, as a necessary consequence, ought to affect incomes from bonds and interest upon the royal funds in the same proportion as land.

It is useless to urge that such an extension of the tax would be a violation of the public faith: property in bonds is no more sacred than property in land: and if the nation can consent to a tax upon one it can also tax the other. The same contribution should be exacted from the emoluments derived from all financial positions and from all lucrative employments.

The order of nobility has no doubt that the national assembly will concern itself with the examination and reformation of that mass of taxes, the collection of which, thanks to the financial spirit which necessity has imparted to the administration, has been rendered intolerable to the people; such as the *gabelle*, the *aides* and others.

While awaiting the suppression of these taxes, their simplification, condensation, conversion or assessment by provinces, we ask that at least their collection be made less burdensome; that lists be drawn up and given to the public, in order that each may know the amount of his obligation; that over-assessments be avoided and abuses reformed.

Of these taxes certain ones have drawn our especial attention, as producing a very moderate contribution to the public treasury, while the inconvenience, the outlay, the expense of collection which they entail are out of proportion to the pecuniary advantages derived from them.

Of such a nature is the tax upon leather, a substance susceptible of contraction and expansion, which has given rise to frequent contentions, to accusations of false marks and to criminal processes.

The provincial assembly of Orléans has already declared against the collection of this tax, and has established the possibility of its conversion. This body has shown that the tax involves the ruin of the leather trade in France, and that we shall not be able, if the tax be continued, to compete with English leathers, either in price or quality.

Of such a character also is the tax of *franc-fief*, which is a burden to the third estate, which pays it; to the nobility, whose estates and rentals it diminishes in value, and to the King himself, who would be more than indemnified, in case the tax were abolished, by the increase in the value of all landed estates that hold from him.

So also with the *capitation*, a vexatious and arbitrary tax, which we hope to see abolished.

So also with the fees accorded to commissioners of appraisement, who conduct public sales in the villages. This tax bears heavily upon inheritances, and it often happens that the proceeds from the sale of the effects of the unhappy country people are not sufficient to discharge the costs of the sale.

So with stamp duties, registry fees and the *centième denier*. The legal status of these taxes is so generally unknown, and so far beyond the comprehension of those who have not made a special study of the matter, that the contributor is necessarily at the mercy of the collector, without it being possible for him to contest the case or defend himself.

It is no doubt useful that there should be legal forms, which fix the date of documents; registers, where they are transcribed and rendered public; but the aggregate of these registry and transcription fees should not exceed the amounts required for the maintenance of officials: these dues should be fixed according to a simpler and more definite scale, available to everybody; and it is difficult to see why a matter of police and public security should be treated as a source of revenue for the state.

In connection with the greater part of the domanial taxes it is a remarkable fact that the intendant is the only judge having jurisdiction over contests arising in their collection, except by appeal to the council; the result is that the commissioner of the king alone may preside as judge in cases of original jurisdiction, and these are determined upon appeal by the king's council.

Of this character also is the tax which results from the exclusive privilege of the stage routes, a privilege enjoyed by the king and farmed out by provinces. At a time when the necessity is keenly felt of encouraging commerce and communication a tax upon travellers is impolitic, and this fact alone should suffice to ensure its suppression. A person travelling on business pays sufficient taxes upon the food he consumes along the route, he contributes adequately to the public expenses in the taxes imposed upon the articles of commerce in which he deals, without the annoyance of an indirect tax, which restricts his liberty and at the same time yields almost nothing to the public treasury.

But in addition to the inconvenience which the farming of stage-routes involves, when regarded as a tax, as an exclusive privilege it presents the greatest objections: it places the traveller at the mercy of a contractor, who is frequently unable to perform his obligation, and who nevertheless assumes a right over those who are willing to perform it in his stead: it delays the traveller and hampers the ease and facility of his communications.

The free and voluntary renunciation which the order of nobility is about to make of its pecuniary privileges gives it the right to demand that no exemption whatsoever shall be retained in favor of any class of citizens. We have no doubt that the clergy will voluntarily consent to bear all taxes in common with citizens of other orders, in proportion to their possessions; and we demand that the privileges of free cities, of stage masters, of sealers of weights and measures and of all other persons be abolished; in order that the tax shall affect all persons and places in proportion to the net product of their incomes.

THE ADMINISTRATION OF JUSTICE.

Art. 3. The order of the nobility of the *bailliage* of Blois will review this subject briefly. We shall limit ourselves to observing that the administration of justice is less a privilege than a duty of sovereignty; that it ought to be gratuitous, at least to the poor, or in any event not expensive; that procedure should be simple and expeditious; that all useless stages of jurisdiction should be abolished; that in arranging the jurisdiction and fixing the competence of courts the convenience of litigants alone should be regarded, and not that of magistrates, since magistrates were constituted for the people and not the people for the magistrates. That certain estimates, which have come to the notice of the nobility of the *bailliage* of Blois, respecting the enormous cost to the nation of the administration of justice, have produced upon us an impression of grief and horror.

That, through a neglect of constitutional principles, all powers of the state have been confounded with the judicial power; that under the pretext of judicial rulings the superior courts have assumed a portion of the legislative power; that under the pretext of police regulations the inferior courts, oftentimes a single person bent upon following out his individual system, have been permitted to establish regulations which encroach upon the liberty of citizens and seriously affect the rights of property.

The attention of the order of nobility has been still more painfully directed to our criminal laws. Originating in a period of ignorance and barbarity, they reflect the ferocity of manners then prevailing. From the moment of his apprehension the accused is looked upon as guilty; counsel and assistance of all kinds are refused him.

A judge of original jurisdiction examines witnesses and receives depositions; and this testimony, received by a judge ofttimes ill instructed, sometimes prejudiced, becomes practically a sentence of death, from which the accused cannot hope to escape; for what assistance can the appellate court provide, when it determines only upon procedure, upon depositions received from the first judge?

It is not the duty of the nobility of the *bailliage* of Blois to attempt to present to the States General a plan for the reformation of the civil and criminal laws. There will not be wanting virtuous, sensible and enlightened magistrates, gathered from all provinces of the kingdom, who will make their voices heard in that august assembly.

We limit ourselves to demand that there shall be appointed, at the opening of the coming assembly of the States General, a commission composed of persons of enlightenment, whose business it shall be to take this matter into consideration. This commission ought not to be composed exclusively of magistrates and jurists; the most distinguished virtue is not beyond the seduction of prejudice. There ought to be included citizens of all estates and orders, particularly of those who have had the privilege of studying the English system of criminal jurisprudence.

We shall not close this article without asking:

1. That legal forms accompanying actions arising from the seizure and sale of property, administrations and creditors' mandates, and other actions in which a large number of persons are interested, shall be abridged and simplified;

2. That the file of notarial records shall be sacred; that they shall be placed, after an interval of time has elapsed, in a public place, where all citizens may have access to them.

3. That there shall be established in each rural parish a court of reconciliation, composed of the *seigneur*, the parish priest and certain elderly men, for the purpose of amicably settling disputes and preventing suits at law.

ADMINISTRATION OF THE DOMAIN AND FORESTS OF THE KING.

Art. 4. The king's domain has ever been regarded as charged with perpetual entail, and according to this principle was not subject to sale, but only to pledges and exchanges. We shall not consider whether these pledges and exchanges have been disadvantageous to the interests of the king, as is the general belief; but the nobility of the *bailliage* of Blois is unwilling to see the patrimony of our kings scattered and swallowed up in the immensity of the public debt.

Certain important considerations make it desirable that the forests shall not be included in the sale of the domain.

A great nation, and especially a maritime nation like France, ought to regard its timber areas as national property, precious for its defence, not to be withdrawn from the control of the sovereign. It is the general opinion that a greater advantage is derived from cutting the young timber than from allowing it to grow to maturity; that the longer this is delayed, the greater is the loss: the desire for enjoyment is a natural sentiment, and common to all mankind; no one will inte himself in a kind of wealth, which will have a real value only in fifth generation. Legal exemptions, government encouragement, all possible means avail nothing against this instinct.

These reflections are sufficient to make it evident that it is necessary either to abandon the idea of protecting the old forests of France, or to put them under the safeguard of the nation. The nobility of the *bailliage* of Blois is of the opinion that all idea of selling or alienating the royal forests ought to be abandoned, and that every attempt of this nature is to be regarded as a public evil.

If then from the property which forms the body of the king's domain the forests, which form a considerable part, be withdrawn, together with that portion already alienated, of which it would perhaps be impossible to regain possession, or the resumption of which would be disadvantageous, the remaining portion subject to sale would afford only a meagre resource and would bear no proportion to the deficit which it is a question of reducing.

As a result of these considerations the nobility of the *bailliage* of Blois is persuaded that in case the States General determine to abandon the principle of the inalienability of the domain, it would be unnecessary to hasten the sale. A large portion of this property has not been brought up to its real value, and it is important, before it is sold, that an effort should be made to improve its condition. We shall limit ourselves then to the request, that at this first session of the States General transactions in respect to the king's domain be subjected to more rigorous conditions; that no disposition be made of the domain until the provincial estates have been consulted, and that final action be reserved for the approbation of the following session of the States General; and that in respect to financial operations and exchanges which have been begun, but not yet confirmed and legally completed, nor appraisement made, revision shall be reserved for the next States General. Moreover in the matter of the forest of Russy, the complaint of the nobility of Blézois and the memorial in reply of Baron d' Espagnac, together with the documents relative thereto, shall be turned over to the deputies, with instructions to put them into the hands of the States General.

We shall also remark that, while awaiting a definite policy in regard to the alienation of the domain and the management of the forests, it is desirable that their control should be entrusted to a permanent administration, resident in the provinces, whose interests must be identical with the king's, and that all these qualifications are found eminently nited in the provincial estates. This new form of administration would be more economical, inasmuch as it would allow the suppression of the offices of inspector of waters and forests, and a part of the present domanial administration.

THE REGULATION OF EXPENDITURE.

Art. 5. One of the most important duties which the States General will be called upon to fulfil, is the regulation of expenditures.

They should reduce expenditures, in each department, to that which is absolutely indispensable. They should demand the abolition of all useless offices, posts and places, especially those which require neither function nor residence: they should reduce all appointments, salaries, rewards, pensions and gratuities which they deem excessive. They should make public the list of pensions; they should inquire into the motives which have actuated their concession: finally, they should not attempt to reduce the deficit by increased taxation, until they have exhausted all means of restoring a balance by measures of economy.

They should adopt most stringent regulations, to the end that the sums voted for the expenses of each department shall in no case be exceeded; that accounts shall be promptly rendered; that all shall be subjected to the same rules and formalities, and that no expenditure shall be made upon the authority of a simple order in council.

In order to quiet still further the apprehension of national creditors, and to establish confidence upon an indestructible basis, the repayments of the capital and interest of the public debt should no longer be made from the royal treasury, but from the treasury of the nation: a portion of the public revenue should be set aside month by month, so that payments may never be deferred, and then it may be truly said that the national debt is consolidated.

They should cause to be printed lists of pensions, gratuities and special gifts, with details of the motives occasioning them. These lists should be revised every year and published as above, together with a general and detailed account of the finances, receipts and expenditures

eral for their administration, in all that relates to the laws of the kingdom.

AGRICULTURE.

Art. 6. Of all classes of citizens none is in a better position to know the needs of agriculture than the nobility, which lives upon the land. The nobility of the *bailliage* of Blois would have reason to reproach itself, if it did not unite, in a special article, the observations of this assembly and the information which it has been able to collect from the minutes of the provincial assembly of Orléans, concerning the agriculture of this province in particular.

Certain calculations, which bear the marks of exactness, and the results of which may be regarded as sufficiently accurate in a matter of this nature, establish the fact that while in England an area of one thousand square toises yields a gross product of 48,000 lbs. a year, the same area in France produces only 18,000 lbs.

It would be useless to seek the cause of this enormous difference in the fertility of the soil. The soil of France is quite as good as that of England, and France has, to a greater degree than England, certain products, peculiar to herself, such as silk, wines, oils etc.

This disproportion has no connection with the characteristics of the two peoples; the French people have neither less courage nor less ingenuity than the English. It is impossible to conceal the fact: it is again a consequence of vices in the constitution. For centuries the country people have groaned under the yoke of pecuniary burdens, the more overwhelming insomuch as they are arbitrary. The terror, which the rigorous collection of taxes has inspired, has driven into the cities all the ability and all the capital, to such a degree that no large speculative enterprise concerns itself with agriculture.

Another cause contributing more than any other to turn capital from agriculture is the high rate of interest, which the demands and frequent loans of the government have occasioned. The allurement of a life of ease, demanding neither care nor labor, has drained the country of money and accumulated it in the towns.

Without considerable advances only a feeble state of agriculture can be obtained; without capital there can be no live stock, without live stock no manure, without manure no crops; and such is the state to which agriculture in parts of this province has been reduced.

The States General will render a most signal service to agriculture, as well as to commerce, by causing to fall, as rapidly as possible, the high rate of interest.

The nobility of the *bailliage* of Blois has dwelt with some emphasis upon these considerations, because it has found here additional motives for strengthening the demand, which it has already expressed, for an abolition of the *taille*, and a general suppression of all arbitrary taxation.

These statements refer principally to the less fertile portions of Beance and Dunois. Sologne presents a picture even more dispiriting: it lies almost wholly in empty pastures; nothing is sown except here and there rye and buckwheat.

Certain investigations made from time to time in regard to the population of this province, seem to show that it is decreasing; and in fact the stagnant waters, which cover it in winter, render residence here unhealthful, producing fevers in autumn, and shortening the average life of the country people: but while the number of persons has decreased, while agriculture has become impoverished, the *taille* has remained ever the same, and it has risen to-day to almost half the revenues of the proprietors.

These details are necessary in order to call attention to the necessity of reducing the burdens of the province, and of opening a canal which shall drain the country.

Dunois demands still more immediate relief, and relief proportionate to its needs. A terrible scourge has ravaged its fields in the past year and destroyed the crops; the spirit of justice demands that independent of indemnities which may be granted, there should be a total remission of taxes to those who have no harvest, and to others in proportion to their loss.

Blézois has just suffered a loss, which cannot be repaired in many years, through the destruction of its vines by frost. Sologne, in the loss of the fish in its ponds, which died from the severe cold. It is impossible that these disasters, which have ruined proprietors, should not diminish the receipts of the public treasury, and the nobility permits itself to hope that these facts will be taken into consideration.

The principal assistance which agriculture awaits at this moment from the representatives of the nation is as follows;

1. Absolute freedom in the sale and circulation of grain and produce;
2. A regulation favoring the redemption of socome and otl

burdensome taxes, the drainage of swamps, the division of communal lands;

3. Government encouragement in the production of better grades of wool and in the breeding of cattle;

4. Abolition of sealers of weights and measures;

5. Establishments for weaving, for the manufacture of the coarser fabrics in the villages, to give employment to the country people during the idle period of the year;

6. Better facilities for the education of children; elementary textbooks, adapted to their capacity, where the rights of man and the social duties shall be clearly set forth;

7. More expert surgeons and experienced midwives, etc.

Deputies ought to find assistance toward these ends in the agricultural societies, in the learned associations of the capital and in the great number of works which have been published in the last few years. They should not lose sight of the fact that agriculture is the foremost of all the arts; that it is the source of reviving prosperity; agriculture it is that furnishes to all manufacturers the raw materials upon which industry is exercised, and to commerce the materials of exchange; it furnishes subsistence to all; and, finally, it is in agriculture that the strength of the nation resides.

SPECIAL MATTERS.

Art. 7. The nobility of the *bailliage* of Blois, in commencing the composition of these instructions, had nothing further in view than the tracing of a plan of constitution most conformable to the principles of monarchy, and most likely to ensure to the nation the free exercise of its legitimate rights; we proposed moreover to confine ourselves to general considerations. The great number of suggestions and memorials, however, which have been sent in by various members of the order during the progress of our labors, has gradually diverted us from our earlier plan, and it seems to us desirable to include a number of felicitous ideas and important reflections, which do honor to the knowledge and patriotic spirit of their originators. Fearing, however, that they might lose somewhat of their original force or be inadequately developed in our presentation, we have determined that the original memorials themselves should be turned over to the deputies. The leading ideas which we have extracted from these writings, and which we have determined to incorporate in our demands, are the following:

1. The augmentation, *out of the funds of the clergy, of the salary of parish priests with minimum dotation*, the greater part of wh   , are in a state bordering so closely upon poverty, that they often share in the misery of the country people, without being able to relieve it.

2. That the law exempting from the payment of *taille* each rural inhabitant who has twelve children be reenacted, and in case of the total suppression of the *taille* some equivalent compensation be made.

3. Throughout the whole kingdom there should be but one code of laws, one system of weights and measures.

4. That a commission be established composed of the most eminent men of letters of the capital and provinces, and citizens of all orders, to formulate a plan of national education for the benefit of all classes of society; and for the purpose of revising elementary text-books.

5. That all customs duties collected in the interior of the kingdom be abolished, and all custom-houses, offices and customs barriers be removed to the frontier.

6. That rank, power or credit shall not be permitted to avert the rigors of the law in the case of fraudulent bankruptcies, and that the custom of issuing writs of suspension be done away with, at least until they have been demanded by the creditors themselves.

7. That any bill signed by a nobleman be declared a bill of honor.

8. That the troops be employed upon the highways and public works.

9. That there be established in country parishes, at the expense of *seigneurs* who demand it, retreats for disabled soldiers, for which the king shall furnish only the clothing.

10. That the law prohibiting all persons not noble from carrying arms be put in force, and that precautions be taken to assure its execution.

11. That the mounted police be increased, and that projects which have been advanced looking to an establishment of foot brigades be considered.

With regard to all that concerns public charities, mendicancy, hospitals, foundling asylums and other benevolent institutions, the assembly of the nobility recognizes their importance, but considers itself not in duty bound to take them into consideratic , since they are more especially within the jurisdiction of the provincial estates.

CONCERNING THE NATIONAL CONSTITUTION AND THE MEANS OF OBTAINING THE ABOLITION OF ABUSES.

Art. 8. Up to this point we have merely indicated the abuses which have accumulated in France during a long succession of centuries; we have made it evident that the rights of citizens have been abridged by a multitude of laws which attack property, liberty and personal safety.

That these rights have suffered injury as well in the nature as in the imposition of the taxes; in the administration of justice in both civil and criminal law; that this has been the case especially in the administration of the public revenues.

It is not sufficient to suppress these abuses; it is necessary to prevent their return; there must be established an ever active influence, moving without interruption in the direction of public prosperity, which shall bear in itself the germ of all good, a principle destructive of all evil.

In order to accomplish this great object the nobility of the *bailliage* of Blois demand:

That the States General about to assemble shall be permanent and shall not be dissolved until the constitution be established; but in case the labors connected with the establishment of the constitution be prolonged beyond a space of two years, the assembly shall be reorganized with new deputies freely and regularly elected.

That a fundamental and constitutional law shall assure forever the periodical assembly of the States General at frequent intervals, in such a manner that they may assemble and organize themselves at a fixed time and place, without the concurrence of any act emanating from the executive power.

That the legislative power shall reside exclusively in the assembly of the nation, under the sanction of the king, and shall not be exercised by any intermediate body during the recess of the States General.

That the king shall enjoy the full extent of executive power necessary to insure the execution of the laws; but that he shall not be able in any event to modify the laws without the consent of the nation.

That the form of the military oath shall be changed, and the troops promise obedience and fidelity to the king and the nation.

That taxes may not be imposed without the consent of the nation;

that taxes may be granted only for a specified time, and for no longer than the next meeting of the States General.

[*The question of how voting should be conducted in the States General called forth a variety of opinions, and it was decided to insert in the cahier the minutes of the meeting of March 28, in so far as they bore upon the matter. The substance of the discussion is as follows:*

Upon the first ballot the assembly stood 51 for the vote by order and 43 for the vote per capita.

It was suggested however that many present favored a mixed system of voting, viz.: that in matters of general welfare, or which involved the granting of subsidies and the maintenance of the national honor, voting should be per capita; that in matters touching the rights and interests of the individual orders, voting should be by order.

Upon ballot, 68 signified their approval of this system and 28 still adhered to the vote by order.]

There shall be established this year, if possible, and before the adjournment of the States General, provincial estates, which shall superintend the levy of taxes approved by the nation, ... have charge of highways and public works and of all that concerns the special local interests of the provinces, as well as all matters of administration confided to them by the States General, especially the administration of the domains and forests belonging to the king and to communes.

With respect to the organization of the provincial estates the nobility of the *bailliage* of Blois will aquiesce in whatever the States General may be pleased to determine.

That a part of the magisterial and judicial powers hitherto possessed by intendants shall be entrusted to a court established in each *généralité*.

It has been determined to grant absolute powers to delegates; but that notice be given them that the unanimous desire of the nobility of the *bailliage* of Blois has never swerved from this principle: No subsidies without a constitution; no tax to be legal, unless decreed and determined by the States General.

[*The cahier is signed by 7 marquises, 7 counts, 3 viscounts, 3 barons, 9 knights, and 64 persons without special title.*]

III. CAHIER,

Of the grievances, complaints and remonstrances of the members of the third estate of the bailliage of Versailles.

Archives Parlementaires, Vol. V, p. 180-185.

CONSTITUTION.

Art. 1. The power of making laws resides in the king and the nation.

Art. 2. The nation being too numerous for a personal exercise of this right, has confided its trust to representatives freely chosen from all classes of citizens. These representatives constitute the national assembly.

Art. 3. Frenchmen should regard as laws of the kingdom those alone which have been prepared by the national assembly and sanctioned by the king.

Art. 4. Succession in the male line and primogeniture are usages as ancient as the monarchy, and ought to be maintained and consecrated by solemn and irrevocable enactment.

Art. 5. The laws prepared by the States General and sanctioned by the king shall be binding upon all classes of citizens and upon all provinces of the kingdom. They shall be registered literally and accurately in all courts of law. They shall be open for consultation at all seats of municipal and communal government; and shall be read at sermon time in all parishes.

Art. 6. That the nation may not be deprived of that portion of legislation which is its due, and that the affairs of the kingdom may not suffer neglect and delay, the States General shall be convoked at least every two or three years.

Art. 7. No intermediate commission of the States General may ever be established, since deputies of the nation have no right to delegate the powers confirmed to them.

Art. 8. Powers shall be conferred upon delegates for one year only; but they may be continued or confirmed by a single reelection.

Art. 9. The persons of deputies shall be inviolable. They may not be prosecuted in civil cases during their term of office; nor held responsible to the executive authorities for any speech made in the assembly; but they shall be responsible to the States General alone.

Art. 10. Deputies of the Third Estate, or their president or speaker, shall preserve the same attitude and demeanor as the representatives of the two upper orders, when they address the sovereign. As regards the three orders there shall be no difference observed in the ceremonial made use of at the convocation of the estates.

Art. 11. Personal liberty, proprietary rights and the security of citizens shall be established in a clear, precise and irrevocable manner. All *lettres de cachet* shall be abolished for ever, subject to certain modifications which the States General may see fit to impose.

Art. 12. And to remove forever the possibility of injury to the personal and proprietary rights of Frenchmen, the jury system shall be introduced in all criminal cases, and in civil cases for the determination of fact, in all the courts of the realm.

Art. 13. All persons accused of crimes not involving the death penalty shall be released on bail within twenty-four hours. This release shall be pronounced by the judge upon the decision of the jury.

Art. 14. All persons who shall have been imprisoned upon suspicion, and afterwards proved innocent, shall be entitled to satisfaction and damages from the state, if they are able to show that their honor or property has suffered injury.

Art. 15. A wider liberty of the press shall be accorded, with this provision alone: that all manuscripts sent to the printer shall be signed by the author, who shall be obliged to disclose his identity and bear the responsibility of his work; and to prevent judges and other persons in power from taking advantage of their authority, no writing shall be held a libel until it is so determined by twelve jurors, chosen according to the forms of a law which shall be enacted upon this subject.

Art. 16. Letters shall never be opened in transit; and effectual measures shall be taken to the end that this trust shall remain inviolable.

Art. 17. All distinctions in penalties shall be abolished; and crimes committed by citizens of the different orders shall be punished irrespectively, according to the same forms of law and in the same manner. The States General shall seek to bring it about that the effects of transgression shall be confined to the individual, and shall not be reflected upon the relatives of the transgressor, themselves innocent of all participation.

Art. 18. Penalties shall in all cases be moderate and proportionate to the crime. All kinds of torture, the rack and the stake, shall be abolished. Sentence of death shall be pronounced only for atrocious crimes and in rare instances, determined by the law.

Art. 19. Civil and criminal laws shall be reformed.

Art. 20. The military throughout the kingdom shall be subject to the general law and to the civil authorities, in the same manner as other citizens.

Art. 21. No tax shall be legal unless accepted by the representatives of the people and sanctioned by the king.

Art. 22. Since all Frenchmen receive the same advantage from the government, and are equally interested in its maintenance they ought to be placed upon the same footing in the matter of taxation.

Art. 23. All taxes now in operation are contrary to these principles and for the most part vexatious, oppressive and humiliating to the people. They ought to be abolished as soon as possible, and replaced by others common to the three orders and to all classes of citizens, without exception.

Art. 24. In case the present taxes are provisionally retained, it should be for a short time, not longer than the session of the States General, and it shall be ordered that the proportional contribution of the two upper orders shall be due from them on the day of the promulgation of the law of the constitution.

Art. 25. After the establishment of the new taxes, which shall be paid by the three orders, the present exceptional method of collecting from the clergy shall be done away with, and their future assemblies shall deal exclusively with matters of discipline and dogma.

Art. 26. All new taxes, real and personal, shall be established only for a limited time, never to exceed two or three years. At the expiration of this term, they shall be no longer collected, and collectors or or other officials soliciting the same shall be proceeded against as guilty of extortion.

Art. 27. The anticipation of future revenues, loans in whatsoever disguise, and all other financial expedients of the kind, of which so great abuse has been made, shall be forbidden.

Art. 28. In case of war, or other exceptional necessity, no loan shall be made without the consent of the States General, and it shall be enacted that no loan shall be effected, without provision being made by taxation for the payment of interest, and of the principal at a specified time.

Art. 29. The amount which each citizen shall be obliged to pay, in case of war, by reason of an increase in the existing taxes, at a certain rate per livre, shall be determined beforehand by the States General in conjunction with the king. The certainty of increase ought to have a marked effect in preventing useless and unjust wars, since it clearly indicates to Frenchmen the new burden they will have to bear, and to foreign nations the resources which the nation has in reserve and at hand to repulse unjust attacks.

Art. 30. The exact debt of the government shall be established by the States General, and after verification it shall be declared the national debt.

Art. 31. Perpetual and life annuities shall be funded at their present value.

Art. 32. The expenses of the departments shall be determined by their actual needs, and so established by a committee of the States General, in such a manner that the expenditures may never exceed the sums appropriated.

Art. 33. There shall be no increase in taxation, until the receipts and expenditures have been compared with the utmost care, and a real deficit discovered; in fact, not until all possible reductions have been made in the expenses of each department.

Art. 34. The expenses of the war department call for the special attention of the States General. These expenses mount annually to the appalling sums of 110 and 120 millions. In order to effect their reduction, the States General shall demand the accounts of this department under the recent ministries, particularly under the ministry of the Duc de Choiseul.

Art. 35. The present militia system, which is burdensome, oppressive and humiliating to the people, shall be abolished; and the States General shall devise means for its reformation.

Art. 36. A statement of Pensions shall be presented to the States General; they shall be granted only in moderate amounts, and then only for services rendered. The total annual expenditure for this purpose should not exceed a fixed sum. A list of pensions should be printed and made public each year.

Art. 37. Since the nation undertakes to provide for the personal expenses of the sovereign, as well as for the crown and state, the law providing for the inalienability of the domain shall be repealed. As a result, all the domanial possessions immediately in the king's possession, as well as those already pledged, and the forests of his majesty. as well, shall be sold, and transferred in small lots, in so far as possible, and always at public auction to the highest bidder; and the proceeds ap plied to the reduction of the public debt. In the meanwhile all woods and forests shall continue to be controlled and administered, whoever may be the actual proprietors, according to the provisions of the law of 1669.

Art. 38. The execution of this law shall be confided to the provincial estates, which shall prosecute violations of the law before judges in ordinary.

Art. 39. Apanages shall be abolished and replaced, in the case of princes who possess them, with cash salaries, which shall be included in the expenses of the crown.

Art. 40. The States General shall take under advisement these transfers which have not yet been verified and completed.

Art. 40. b. Ministers and all government officials shall be responsible to the States General for their conduct of affairs. They may be impeached according to fixed forms of law and punished according to the statute.

Art. 41. All general and particular statements and accounts relative to the administration shall be printed and made public each year.

Art. 42. The coinage may not be altered without the consent of the Estates; and no bank established without their approval.

Art. 43. A new subdivision shall be made of the provinces of the realm; provincial estates shall be established, members of which, not excepting their presidents, shall be elected.

Art. 44. The constitution of the provincial estates shall be uniform throughout the kingdom, and fixed by the States General. Their powers shall be limited to the interior administration of the provinces, under the supervision of his majesty, who shall communicate to them the national laws which have received the consent of the States General and the royal sanction: to which laws all the provincial estates shall be obliged to submit without reservation.

Art. 45. All members of the municipal assemblies of towns and villages shall be elected. They may be chosen from all classes of citizens. All municipal offices, now existing, shall be abolished; and their redemption shall be provided for by the States General.

Art. 46. All offices and positions, civil, ecclesiastical and military, shall be open to all orders; and no humiliating and unjust exception (in the case of the third estate), destructive to emulation and injurious to the interests of the state, shall be perpetuated.

Art. 47. The right of *aubaine* shall be abolished with regard to all nationalities. All foreigners, after three years residence in the kingdom, shall enjoy the rights of citizenship.

Art. 48. Deputies of French colonies in America and in the Indies, which form an important part of our possessions, shall be admitted to the States General, if not at the next meeting, at least at the one following.

Art. 49. All relics of serfdom, agrarian or personal, still remaining in certain provinces, shall be abolished.

Art. 50. New laws shall be made in favor of the negroes in our colonies; and the States General shall take measures toward the abolition of slavery. Meanwhile let a law be passed, that negroes in the colonies who desire to purchase their freedom, as well as those whom their masters are willing to set free, shall no longer be compelled to pay a tax to the domain.

Art. 51. The three functions, legislative, executive and judicial, shall be separated and carefully distinguished.

The communes of the bailliage of Versailles have already expressed themselves in respect to the necessity of adopting the form of deliberation *per capita* in the coming States General. The reform of the constitution will be one of their principal duties. This magnificent monument of liberty and public felicity should be the work of the three orders in common session; if they are separated, certain pretensions, anxieties and jealousies are bound to arise; the two upper orders are likely to oppose obstacles, perhaps invincible, to the reform of abuses and the enactment of laws destined to suppress such abuses. It seems indispensable that in this first assembly votes should be taken *per capita* and not by order. After the renunciation by the two upper orders of their pecuniary privileges; after all distinctions before the law have been abolished; when the exclusion of the third estate from certain offices and positions has been done away with,—then the reasons which to-day necessitate deliberation *per capita* will no longer exist.

The communes of Versailles therefore refrain from expressing a positive opinion upon the future composition of the national assemblies and upon the method of their deliberation. They defer, with all confidence, the decision of this important question to the wisdom of the States General.

Our prayer is that the methods determined upon shall be such as will assure forever, to the king and to the nation those portions of the legislative power which respectively belong to them; that they shall maintain between them a perfect equilibrium in the employment of this power; that they shall conserve, forever, to the nation its rights and liberties; to the king his prerogatives and the executive power in all its fulness. Finally that these methods should be so combined as to produce that circumspectness and lack of haste so necessary to the enactment of laws, and that they will effectually prevent all hasty counsels, dissentions amongst deputies and immature conclusions.

May all deputies to this august assembly, impressed with the sanctity and extent of their obligations, forget that they are the mandatories of some special order, and remember only that they are representatives of the people. May they never be forgetful of the fact, that they are about to fix the destinies of the foremost nation of the world!

THE EXECUTIVE.

Art. 52. It shall be ordained by the constitution that the executive power be vested in the king alone.

Art. 53. The king shall dispose of all offices, places and positions, ecclesiastical, civil and military, to which he has at present the right of appointment.

Art. 54. All the provincial estates, or commissions representing them, shall receive his immediate orders which it shall be their duty to obey provisionally.

Art. 55. His consent shall be necessary to all bills approved by the States General in order that they may acquire the force of law throughout the realm. He may reject all bills presented to him, without being obliged to state the reasons of his disapproval.

Art. 56. He shall have the sole right of convening, prorogueing and dissolving the States General.

THE JUDICIARY.

Art. 57. The sale of the judicial office shall be suppressed as soon as circumstances will permit, and provision made for the indemnification of holders.

Art. 58. There shall be established in the provinces as many superior courts as there are provincial estates. They shall be courts of final jurisdiction.

Art. 59. All exceptional and privileged seignorial courts shall be abolished, as well as other courts rendered useless by the abolition of certain taxes which caused their erection, and by the adoption of a new system of accounts under the exclusive control of the States General.

Art. 60. All rights of *committimus* or of evocation, which tend to favor certain classes of citizens to the detriment of the general public, shall be abolished.

Art. 61. There shall be only two stages of jurisdiction.

Art. 62. Since the adoption of the jury system will have a tendency to facilitate and simplify the administration of justice, all classes of judges shall be reduced to the least number possible.

Art. 63. Each judge of the lower courts and of the superior provincial courts shall be appointed by the king out of a list of three candidates, presented by the provincial estates.

Art. 64. Judges of all courts shall be obliged to adhere to the letter of the law and may never be permitted to change, modify or interpret it at their pleasure.

Art. 65. The fees received by all officers of justice shall be fixed at a moderate rate and clearly understood; and judges who extort fees in excess of the fixed rates shall be condemned to pay a fine of four times the amount they have received.

Such are the bases of a constitution founded upon the eternal principles of justice and reason, which alone ought to regulate henceforward the government of the realm. Once they are adopted, all false pretensions, all burdensome privileges, all abuses of all kinds will be seen to disappear. Already a considerable number of *bailliages* have expressed their desires concerning the reforms and abolitions to be effected in all branches of the administration; the necessity for these drastic changes has been so evident that it is sufficient merely to indicate them.

GENERAL DEMANDS.

Art. 66. The deputies of the *prévôté* and *vicomté* of Paris shall be instructed to unite themselves with the deputies of other provinces, in order to join with them in securing, as soon as possible, the following abolitions:

    Of the *taille*;
    Of the *gabelle*;
    Of the *aides*;
    Of the *corvée*;
    Of the *ferme* of tobacco;
    Of the registry-duties;

Of the free-hold tax;
Of the taxes on leather;
Of the government stamp upon iron;
Of the stamps upon gold and silver;
Of the interprovincial customs duties;
Of the taxes upon fairs and markets;

Finally, of all taxes that are burdensome and oppressive, whether on account of their nature or of the expense of collection, or because they have been paid almost wholly by agriculturists and by the poorer classes. They shall be replaced with other taxes, less complicated and easier of collection, which shall fall alike upon all classes and orders of the state without exception.

Art. 67. We demand also the abolition of the royal preserves (*capitaineries*);

Of the game laws;
Of jurisdictions of *prévôtés*;
Of *banalités*;
Of tolls;
Of useless authorities and governments in cities and provinces.

Art. 68. We solicit the establishment of public granaries in the provinces, under the control of the provincial estates, in order that by accumulating reserves during years of plenty, famine and excessive dearness of grain, such as we have experienced in the past may be prevented.

Art. 69. We solicit also the establishment of free schools in all country parishes.

Art. 70. We demand, for the benefit of commerce, the abolition of all exclusive privileges:

The removal of customs barriers to the frontiers;
The most complete freedom in trade;
The revision and reform of all laws relative to commerce;
Encouragement for all kinds of manufacture: viz. premiums, bounties and advances:
Rewards to artisans and laborers for useful inventions.

The communes desire that prizes and rewards shall always be preferred to exclusive privileges, which extinguish emulation and lessen competition.

Art. 71. We demand the suppression of various hindrances, such as stamps, special taxes, inspections; and the annoyances and visitations, to which many manufacturing establishments, particularly tanneries, are subjected.

Art. 72. The States General are entreated to devise means for abolishing gild organizations, indemnifying the holders of masterships; and to fix by law the conditions, under which the arts, trades and professions may be followed, without the payment of an admission tax, and at the same time to provide that public security and confidence be undisturbed.

Art. 73. Deputies shall solicit the abolition of:
Receivers of consignments;
Pawn-brokers;
All lotteries;
The bank of Poissy;[1]
All taxes, of whatsoever nature, on grain and flour;
All franchises and exemptions enjoyed by post-agents, except a pecuniary indemnity which shall be accorded them;
The exclusive privilege of the transportation companies, which shall be allowed to continue their public service, in competition, however, with all private companies, which shall see fit to establish public carriages; and these moreover shall be encouraged.

Art. 74. They shall demand complete freedom of transport for grain among the various provinces of the kingdom, without interference from any court whatsoever.

Art. 75. They shall demand also the total abolition of all writs of suspension and of safe conducts.

Art. 76. Superior courts shall be absolutely prohibited from arresting, in any manner whatsoever, by means of decrees or decisions obtained upon petitions not made public, the execution of notarial writs or the decisions of judges of original jurisdiction, when the law shall ordain their provisional execution; under penalty that the judge shall be responsible for the amount of the debt, payment of which he has caused to be arrested.

Art. 77. The abolition of all places of refuge for debtors.

Art. 78. That no merchant or trader may be admitted to any

---

[1] The Bank of Poissy, established in the seventeenth century, acted as an intermediary between the butchers of Paris and outside cattle dealers, furnishing money to the butchers for their purchases. The result, at least in the popular mind, was to raise the price of butchers' wares. This institution had been abolish by Turgot in 1776 and reestablished in 1779.

national assembly or any municipal body, who has demanded abatement from his creditors; still less if he is a fraudulent bankrupt; and he may not be re-established in his rights until he has paid the whole amount of his indebtedness.

Art. 79. That individuals who have issued promissory notes shall be liable to detention.

Art. 80. That the States General shall consider means of diminishing mendicancy.

Art. 81. That civil and military offices may not be held simultaneously by the same person, and that each citizen may hold only one office.

Art. 82. That all the honorary rights of nobles shall be maintained; but that they shall be allowed to hunt only upon their own lands, and not upon the lands of their vassals or tenants.

Art. 83. That nobility may be acquired neither through office or by purchase.

Art. 84. That inheritances shall be divided equally among co-heiritors of the same degree, without regard to sex or right of primogeniture, nor to the status of the co-participants, and without distinction between nobles and non-nobles.

Art. 85. That all entails shall be limited to one generation.

Art. 86. That day laborers may not be taxed to exceed the amount of one day's labor.

Art. 87. That there shall be established in all towns and country parishes commissions of arbitration, composed of a certain number of citizens elected and renewed annually, to which persons may apply and secure provisional judgment, without expense, except in case of appeal to to the regular courts.

Art. 88. That all state prisons shall be abolished, and that means shall be taken to put all other prisons in better sanitary condition.

Art. 89. That it may please the States General to provide means for securing a uniformity of weights and measures throughout the kingdom.

Art. 90. That the laws upon *lods* and *ventes* shall be examined and rendered uniform throughout the kingdom.

Art. 91. That parishes shall be furnished with power to redeem the tax upon the transfer of land.

Art. 92. That *dimes* shall be suppressed and converted into a money rent based upon the price of corn and of the mark of silver, rising proportionately with the combined increase in value of corn and of the mark of silver.

Art. 93. Since clergymen in general ought not to occupy themselves with worldly affairs, there ought to be provided for bishops, archbishops and all holders of benefices a decent income and one suitable to their dignity: accordingly the property of the church in each province ought to be sold under the supervision of the provincial estates, which shall assume the duty of paying to holders of benefices the sums accorded to them by the States General.

Art. 94. That in case the above change should not be made, then it shall be ordained that no clergymen may hold two benefices at the same time, and that all persons now possessing two or more benefices shall be obliged to choose and to declare, within a prescribed time, which one of them they desire to retain.

Art. 95. That all commendatory abbacies, benefices without functions and useless convents shall be suppressed, their possessions sold for the benefit of the state, and the funds thus realized made to constitute an endowment, the income of which shall be used for the benefit of country parish priests for the establishment of free schools, hospitals and other charitable institutions.

Art. 96. That continuous residence of archbishops and bishops in their dioceses and of beneficiaries in their benefices shall be required; and that resignations be not permitted.

Art. 97. That no clergyman under the age of twenty-five may be promoted to a sub-diaconate.

Art. 98. That girls may not enter religious orders until after they are twenty-five years of age, nor men until after thirty.

Art. 99. That it be forbidden to go to the Roman Curia for provisions, nominations, bulls and dispensations of all kinds; and each bishop in his diocese shall have full powers in these matters.

Art. 100. That the right of the pope to grant livings in France be suppressed.

Art. 101. That the Concordat be revoked, and all intervention on the part of the Roman Curia be made to cease.

Art. 102. That loans, contracted by the clergy to cover their contribution to the taxes which they were bound to support, shall be paid by them, since these loans are the obligation of the order; but loans which have been contracted on the government's account shall be included in the royal debt, and added to the national debt.

VARIOUS MATTERS.

Art. 1. Deputies of the *prévôté-vicomté* shall be instructed to demand increased pay for soldiers.

Art. 2. That inhabitants of towns and rural places be paid and indemnified for troops of war quartered upon them, for the transportation of troops and of military baggage.

Art. 3. That the ordinances concerning the king's guard be revised, particularly those clauses which abolish the wise provision of Louis XIV. for the safety of his person, and the regulations made by him relative to his body-guard.

Art. 4. That barbarous punishments, taken from the codes of foreign nations and introduced into the new military regulations, be abolished, and replaced with regulations more in conformity with the genius of the nation.

(*Articles 5, 6, and 7 relate to notarial and registry fees.*)

Art. 8. That it be permitted to contract loans by means of bills or short-term certificates of debt, bearing interest at the legal rate, without it being necessary to alienate the capital so pledged.

Art. 9. In case the property of the church be not sold, that leases shall be continued by the successors of the present holders; at least that they shall not suffer a reduction of more that one-third.

Art. 10. That canals be constructed in all provinces of the kingdom where they will be useful.

Art. 11. That the working of mines be encouraged.

Art. 12. That a new schedule be made of the expenses of funerals, marriages and other church functions.

Art. 13. That cemeteries be located outside of cities, towns and villages; that the same be done with places of deposit for refuse.

Art. 14. That the funds for the support of the lazarettos, formerly located in rural parishes, having been united with the endowments of hospitals, country people shall be permitted to send their sick to the city hospitals.

Art. 15. That the laws of the kingdom shall be equally the laws of the French colonies.

Art. 16. That all kinds of employment suitable for women shall be reserved for them by special enactment.

SERIES FOR 1894.

I. Early Reformation Period in England.* Single number, 20 pages.
II. Urban and the Crusaders.* Single number, 24 pages.
III. The Reaction after 1815.* Single number, 24 pages.
IV. Letters of the Crusaders.* Double number, 40 pages.
V. The French Revolution, 1789–1791.* Double number, 36 pages.
VI. English Constitutional Documents.* Double number, 36 pages.

SERIES FOR 1895.

I. English Towns and Gilds. Double number, 40 pages.
II. Napoleon and Europe. Double number, 32 pages.
III. The Mediaeval Student. Single number, 20 pages.
IV. Monastic Tales of the XIII Century. Single number, 20 pages.
V. England in the Time of Wycliffe. Single number, 20 pages.
VI. Period of Early Reformation in Germany. Double number, 32 pages.
VII. Life of St. Columban. Double number, 36 pages.

SERIES FOR 1896.

I. The Fourth Crusade. Single number, 20 pages.
II. Statistical Documents of the Middle Ages. Single number, 23 pages.
III. Period of the Later Reformation. Double number, 32 pages.
IV. The Witch-Persecutions. Double number, 36 pages.
V. English Manorial Documents. Double number, 32 pages.
VI. The Pre-Reformation Period. Double number, 34 pages.

SERIES FOR 1897.

I. The Early Christian Persecutions. Double number, 32 pages.
II. Canons and Creeds of the First Four Councils. Double number, Dec.
III. Documents Illustrative of Feudalism. Double number, December.
IV. Ordeals, Compurgation, Excommunication, and Interdict. Double number, 34 pages.
V. Typical Cahiers of 1789. Double number, 36 pages.

Annual subscription, $1.00.
Single numbers, Vol. I, 15 cents; Vols. II, III and IV, 10 cents.
Double numbers, Vol. I, 25 cents; Vols. II, III and IV, 20 cents.
Bound Volumes, $1.50.
Discounts will be given on orders for 25 or more numbers.
Subscriptions and orders should be sent to

DANA C. MUNRO,

UNIVERSITY OF PENNSYLVANIA,

November, 1897. Philadelphia, Pa.

* Revised edition.

www.ingramcontent.com/pod-product-compliance
Lightning Source LLC
Chambersburg PA
CBHW030334170426
43202CB00010B/1124